Josep Maria Jujol
Five Major Buildings

SITES/Lumen Books
446 West 20 Street
New York, NY 10011
(212) 989-7944

© 1994 Dennis L. Dollens
ISBN 0-930829-35-2
Printed in the United States of America
Design: D.L. Dollens

SITES Books and Lumen Books are produced by Lumen, Inc., a tax-exempt, non-profit organization. This publication is made possible, in part, with public funds from the New York State Council on the Arts, and private contribubtions.

All phtotographs, unless otherwise noted, are by Ronald Christ and Dennis Dollens.

Photos on pages i, iv, v, 106, and back cover show acid-etched marble floor tiles from Ermita del Roser.

Calligraphic designs and texts on pages iii, 35, 37, 59, 100 are redrawn or traced from photographs. Architectural drawings on pages 76, 85, and the back cover are courtesy of the Col.legi d'Arquitectes de Catalunya.

CONTENTS

For Ronald Christ

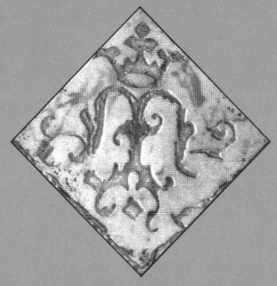

Josep Maria Jujol
Five Major Buildings

Preface

To a great extent the architecture of Josep Maria Jujol, when known at all, has been linked to and explained as a variation of Antoni Gaudí's. We know that Jujol worked as a trusted designer for Gaudí, contributing some of the most admired elements of the master's work. Almost unknown outside of his native Catalunya, however, are his independent buildings, renovations, and interiors. Yet these works are important to anyone interested in early twentieth-century modernism and illuminate little-acknowledged expressionist works and aspects of *modernisme*,[1] the Catalan art movement that roughly parallels art nouveau. I hope the view presented here stimulates questions concerning the completeness as well as the prejudices of twentieth-century architectural history and its northern bias toward pure or classic modernism.

Jujol's life and career spanned nearly seventy-five years, from the late nineteenth century to mid-twentieth, and took in or was susceptible to influences of concurrent fashions, politics, and economics. No objective account or critical biography of the architect in this period exists, and little anecdotal information that is reliable exists outside of *La arquitectura de J. Ma. Jujol* by the architect's son, Josep Maria Jujol, Jr. (and even some of the anecdotes there have been questioned). That work has been translated by Ronald Christ for SITES Books and is currently in production. Its publication makes information, reminiscences, and personal observations available to anyone interested in a view of the architect's work and life. It is the most important and basic work on Jujol and likely to remain so, since all others must, in some basic sense, proceed from it.

Ignasi de Solà-Morales's *Jujol* is an important contribution to Jujol scholarship. Solà-Morales brings his critical mind to bear on Jujol's whole body of work but confines himself primarily to surveying and introducing the architect. Josep Llinàs and Jordi Sarrà's *Josep Maria Jujol* is also a general introduction, beautifully illustrated. I suggest that the reader look to either of these volumes to appreciate Jujol's use of color and to gain an idea of his design spectrum. Joan Bassegoda i Nonell's small book, *Jujol*, is also a source for important biographical information. Various authors contribute insight,

1

analysis, and appreciation to Jujol's work in *Josep Maria Jujol, Arquitecte, 1879-1949*, a special double issue of *Quaderns* (179-180) published by the Col.legi Oficial d'Arquitectes de Catalunya. The single major investigation of the relationship between Jujol and Gaudí in the context of *modernisme* is Carlos Flores's fully illustrated, two volume *Gaudí, Jujol y el Modernismo Catalan*, which establishes an architectural history and is the only work to accept Jujol, Jr.'s invitation to a full-dress scholarly study on the basis of his admittedly preliminary, though undeniably firsthand, account of Jujol's life and work. In addition I would like to note that Sr. Flores championed Jujol in the pages of *Hogar y Arquitectura* early in his tenure as its editor, and to its pages I recommend anyone interested in Jujol as well as modernism in Spain.

Expanding this sparsely, somewhat haphazardly populated range of enthusiasm, I propose to consider five Jujol works, his most important projects, that I believe place him in the front ranks of European modernism. Only as necessary will I discuss projects that lead to or follow these works, and I will not analyze his religion or politics. Still, to sketch the social and artistic context that these five buildings sprang from, I will touch upon Jujol's early life, education, and projects as well as upon some of his late decorative commissions, since these illuminate the architect's consistent style and show how fully he developed a triangulated architecture coded by collage and calligraphy. But, in the main, I aim to determine the major works in the Jujol cannon, itself a spectrum ranging from trivia to masterpieces, and to distinguish the relative quality among his great works. Let me say in advance that while fully cooperating with the increasing international tendency to recognize Jujol, indeed, having collaborated in pioneering efforts to accomplish this recognition, I believe that we do Jujol's work greatest honor, now, by addressing critically the stature and nature of his achievement.

My research into Jujol began in 1979 with the buildings themselves: visits and photographic records. As I realized the extent to which Jujol was not well known in Barcelona and nearly unknown outside that city, I began with my partner Ronald Christ, to document individual projects for SITES magazine and other publications. With the information we discovered and collected from Jujol's family, the owners of buildings, ex-students, and historians we prepared an introduction and guide to the architect's work, SITES 11—the first such publication in English. During the early '80s we also organized three photographic exhibitions of Jujol's work in the United States: in New York at the New York Public Library and the Spanish Institute, and in Chicago, at the Graham Foundation. Our work up to this point logically led to our videotape *Text/ Tiles, Jujol/Gaudí, Bench/Park Güell.*

Throughout this period, we maintained contact with Josep Maria Jujol, Jr., and sometimes met with him in the family residence on Rambla Catalunya. In a parlor, adjacent to the architect's studio, we were surrounded with Jujol's drawings, photographs, and furniture. Sr. Jujol generously offered information and guidance, for which I am grateful. I also think this the appropriate place to note that Sr. Jujol deserves the most credit for keeping his father's reputation alive during those obscure years after 1949.

From our first Barcelona encounter with Jujol's work and continuing to the present, we have been aided, alerted, and informed by friends, friends of friends, and officials known by friends or friends of friends. Some, to our minds, have done heroic feats in literally and figuratively unlocking doors, thus making this ongoing project possible. They include Antoni Muntadas, Carlos Flores, Gregory Kolovakos, Joan Bassegoda i Nonell, George Collins, Lydia Oliva, Antoni Mercader, Antoni Miralda, Elena Bosch, Maite Manye, Catalina Parra, Mireia Sentís, Dore Ashton, Remo Balcells, Monsterrat Duran, Josep Llinàs, Inmaculada Hapsburgo, Enric Cammats, Alfonso Pérez-Méndez, David Ashen, and Laura Starrett.

Lastly, I happily express my special appreciation for the encouragement and financial support of the Architecture, Planning and Design Program at the New York State Council on the Arts. The program's staff, Anne Van Ingen and Deborah Norden, provided early encouragement and program guidance for our efforts to introduce Jujol's work to New York and, eventually, to broader audiences in the United States. Comparably, I want to thank the Col.legi d'Arquitectes de Catalunya, which provided archival and source information as well as contacts. Lastly, proverbially as well as accurately, the graciousness and hospitality of the City of Barcelona merits warmest thanks.

Notes

[1.] A note on proper names: Whenever possible I have used the Catalan for individuals, buildings, streets, projects, etc., which is what the reader will come upon in Barcelona and in scholarship coming out of the region. For example, *Antoni* for *Antonio, modernisme* for *modernismo,* and *can* for *casa.* Yet no rule will govern all situations: Gaudí's monuments, for example, are labeled Casa Milà and Casa Batilló in current Catalan publications, where we also find Jujol's Casa Planells referred alongside his Can Negre. I have striven for a reasonable consistency, one no more variable than the linguistic reality of Catalunya today.

Introduction

I

Whatever other affinities Antoni Gaudí would develop—personal, artistic, or religious—Josep Maria Jujol's future mentor was favorably disposed to the younger architect by virtue of his birthplace, the city of Tarragona, only a short distance from Reus, Gaudí's presumed birthplace. Born on September 16, 1879, Jujol lived and began his education in the ancient Roman city. A story told by his son relates that at an early age Jujol had access and freedom to explore the Cathedral of Tarragona, where he discovered banners, inscriptions, and decorative motifs. The precise articles or motifs are not documented, nor are the effects of his youthful discoveries on his later work, but it is likely that his use of the Marian heart and the tau cross, both decorative symbols found in the cathedral, originate from this period. We may further speculate that his use of other religious and cryptic symbols, as well varied calligraphic styles, stems, at least partially, from these encounters. In addition to the cathedral and its works, during these years Jujol became familiar with, and an admirer of, the city's spectacular Roman ruins and its Romanesque monuments.

    In 1888 the Jujol family moved from Tarragona to a then unincorporated section of Barcelona, Gràcia, and over the course of the next few years moved several times within the city. In addition to his regular schooling during this period, Jujol took private drawing lessons, and by 1897 the eighteen-year-old student enrolled in the Barcelona School of Architecture. In 1901, while still a student, he began working for the prominent architect Antoni Gallissà. While with Gallissà, he was involved in various aspects of the architect's work, notably, the decorative sgraffiti depicting St. Antoni in Gallissà's own house. Surely it was while working on this project that Jujol began to master this craft, which he would later employ so often and expressively on his own buildings. From this elaborate work in the entrance of Gallissà's house we can mark Jujol's future consistent use of the wall as textual and decorative tablet.

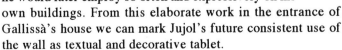

    Between 1903 and 1905, and before graduating, Jujol worked for another prominent Catalan architect, Josep Font i

5

Gumà, with whom he collaborated on the Ateneu Barcelonès. At some point in these years Jujol joined Gaudí's workshop. The precise date when he began working for Gaudí is unclear, but it is generally thought to be sometime between 1904 and early 1906. On May 18, 1906, Jujol was awarded his architectural degree and two years later he opened his own practice, while still maintaining close personal and working ties with Gaudí. In May 1909 he started his teaching career, which, with the exception of a period during the Civil War, he would continue in for forty years, until his death in 1949.

II

Concurrent with Jujol's architectural education and early employment, Barcelona experienced its first exposure to the avant-garde movements of the twentieth century. In 1898, Els Quatre Gats, the cafe that was to become one of the major meeting places for the city's artists, opened, and by 1899 was being frequented by Picasso, Isidre Nonell, Ramon Casas, and other modern painters, sculptors, and writers. In 1900 Picasso mounted his first one-man show in the cafe.

In the following two decades, a period when Jujol moved from apprentice to independent architect, avant-garde activity continued in Barcelona. A member of the Quatre Gats circle, Josep Dalmau, opened Galeries Dalmau in 1906 and initiated his historic series of exhibitions that included, by the time Jujol was entering his most creative period, an exhibition of Picasso's blue period followed by Duchamp's cubist works. In 1916 Dalmau showed Robert and Sonia Delaunay and later Joaquín Torres García (whom Jujol may have known since Torres García worked for Gaudí on the Cathedral of Mallorca). The following year, another member of the international avant-garde, Francis Picabia, published four issues of his magazine *391* in Barcelona; and, later that year, Diaghilev's Ballets Russes appeared at the Liceu. The first one-man show of Catalunya's native son, Miró, appeared at Dalmau in 1918.

This chronology could be continued through the next decade and even into the 1930s, but its purpose is neither to document Els Quatre Gats as an agent in the early propagation of the avant-garde nor to suggest that Jujol was part of it. Surely he was not. (Though in private conversations the architect's son has emphasized that his father was abreast of current art movements, chiefly through periodicals.) This chronological listing tends to illustrate possible sources and influences available in Barcelona during Jujol's formative and early professional years, influences that would have been difficult to ignore, even though Jujol was more disposed to such groups as the Cercle Artístic de Sant Lluc, founded in 1893.

This traditional Catholic organization, with Gaudí among its founders, was constituted in opposition to perceived decadent and anticlerical modernists. We know that in 1910 Jujol designed a banner for the organization. We do not know whether he separated his adherence to conservative Catholicism from his intellectual and artistic inquisitiveness, or if he indeed had intellectual and artistic needs not nearly or fully satisfied through his own spiritualism, his deep-rooted belief in tradition, and his exposure to Gaudí. His work indicates that with the exception of Gaudí's influence he was a practitioner of a nearly self-generated modernism that occasionally incorporated, or independently replicated, elements of mainstream design. Still it is not known to what degree he studied or tolerated modern movements — cubism, expressionism, surrealism — whose philosophical views were ambivalent or opposed to the Church.

Between 1913 and 1923 Jujol enjoyed his most significant creative period. In five small commissions — Torre de la Creu, Can Negre, Can Bofarull, Church of Vistabella, and Casa Planells, all dating from this ten-year span — we find his most artistically challenging, historically important, and architecturally interesting work — an astonishingly small body of architecture on which to base a claim of greatness for the architect. Nevertheless during this period Jujol was one of the most creative architects working in Catalunya, perhaps in Europe. The great Catalan architects of the nineteenth and early twentieth-century, Domènech i Montaner and the younger Puig i Cadafalch had already created their masterpieces. Gaudí was concentrating on Sagrada Família, foregoing further secular commissions. Architects of Coderch and Sert's generation were still youths or in school (in fact, Coderch was a student of Jujol's).

In this period, Jujol's works breathed with structural inventiveness, abstract forms, and fragmented, collagelike decoration. These few buildings came alive in form and iconography in a manner totally different from that of his predecessors' or contemporaries' work, avoiding the heaviness that burdens most Catalan projects of this period as well as the self-consciousness of Catalan *renaixença* architecture, which set out to glorify a nationalistic past. Today these five works still possess the aura of an inventive and experimenting architect.

Yet, after these projects were completed and larger ones halted or never begun, the years following 1923 saw the beginning of Jujol's eclipse. Exceptions that promised to lift the architect's sagging career out of a downturn are often interesting, but they never achieved the brilliance of his earlier work.

III

Catalunya, like much of Europe during the last decades of the nineteenth century, witnessed a resurgence of nationalism. This nationalism typically found expression in the arts and architecture through the movement known as the *renaixença*, which attempted to assert national ideals through the revival of local history, most notably in stylistic devices quoting Catalan Gothic and Renaissance forms. *Renaixença* buildings look like a bumpy Catalan synthesis of neo-Gothic and High Victorian, and the successor style, a locally pervasive movement related to art nouveau, *modernisme*, comes as a relief. This later populist style has been described as "a coherent movement with . . . two quite marked characteristics: first its incredible diffusion and popularity, and second, its great stylistic complexity, which permitted its compatibility with the revivals."[1] It is through *modernisme*, manifested not only in architecture, but in graphics, music, literature, and fashion, that the spirit of an artistic Catalan identity permeated all social strata and, as we will see, was partially kept alive by Josep Maria Jujol long after its academically assigned death.

In architecture, *modernisme* exuberantly exploited the integration of forms with traditional crafts, especially ceramics, stained glass, and wrought iron; and, like the *renaixença*, it sometimes called on allegorical sculpture, quoting Gothic and/or Romanesque sources. Exemplary works include Domènech i Montaner's Palau de la Música Catalana (1905-08) and his Hospital de Saint Pau (1902-10) as well as Puig i Cadafalch's Casa Amatller (1898-1900), Casa de las Punxes

Hospital de Saint Pau

(1904-1905), and Casa Martí (1896)—the home of Els Quatre Gats. These works should be seen as the forefront of architectural design from which Gaudí and Jujol broke away.

Eclipsing *modernisme*, a successor style, *noucentisme*, falls between the former's height (roughly 1888 to 1914) and the early and mid-1930s height of the GATCPAC.[2] Based on a Mediterranean, stripped neoclassicism, *noucentisme* anticipated the rationalism of the international style, though it was infused (like it predecessors) with monumentalism and ambitions to inspire nationalism, much like the contemporary Italian movement *novecento*. In a personal manner, especially in his late works, Jujol merged the effloration of *modernisme* with a formalized, though impure, *noucentisme*. By doing so, he extended the limits of these two styles and created a body of contemporary work that at times looks eclectic. Yet Jujol's stylistic merger created a parasitic, hybridized style where the underpinnings of rationalism served as a life-support system for the near corpse of *modernisme*.

IV

Perhaps nowhere outside the Weimer Republic did political upheaval play a more integral part in artistic life than in Catalunya. After the brief stability and prosperity following Spain's neutral status during WW I, Spain and Catalunya experienced near-ongoing turmoil. And Barcelona's political climate and hence its artistic atmosphere changed abruptly after Premo de Rivera's resignation as the Spanish dictator on January 29, 1930. With the subsequent declaration of a Spanish Republic, Barcelona's political autonomy from Madrid became a reality. A leftward political shift resulted in more liberal provincial and city governments and corresponded with the founding of GATCPAC.[3] With the fortunate coming together of new leftist politics and the GATCPAC, a sympathetic relationship was established where design was intended to express and help reform society through new architectural and urban forms. Commissions designed in a Mediterraneanized international style were directed to Catalan GATEPAC members who, heavily influenced by Le Corbusier, were guided by his young Catalan disciple, Josep Lluís Sert (as well as by Sert's collaborators and contemporaries Torres Calvé, Sixt Yllescas, and Joan B. Subirana).

With a prevailing liberal government and a semioffi-
cial architecture of modernism, Jujol was in a poor position to
compete for or receive municipal work. And with the Church
under heavy criticism, and at times literally under attack, few
works were channeled to an architect whose monogram incorporated a cross and who had asserted his religious dedication.
(Once he told a student: "You're lucky to have a 't' in your
name. That way, every time you write your signature, you can
make a cross without anybody asking why."[4]) Between 1930
and the outbreak of the Civil War, Jujol received commissions
only for minor restorations and decoration. In 1936, when the
Civil War began, he received no commissions at all.

According to his son, during the war Jujol took the
dangerous action of providing shelter for priests and nuns flee-
ing Republican persecution, hiding them in the family flat on
Rambla Catalunya (one priest was sheltered for a year). In addition to the devastation war inflicted on the architect's career,
further hardship came in August 1936 when he was dismissed
from his teaching job at the technical school, where he gave
classes in crafts associated with architecture. Then, though he
was not dismissed, the School of Architecture itself was closed,
thereby denying him his last means for supporting his family.
Finally, after periods of deprivation, work came from an ex-
student, who shared a project, and Jujol became a supervising
architect for the Agupació Collectiva de la Construcció, a position that required him to survey and sketch Barcelona's war-
damaged buildings and report on the feasibility of their repair.
Scarcely a year later the Republic was defeated, the war ended,
and General Franco was Spain's dictator—and no friend of
Catalunya or Barcelona.

Gauging from the heavy damages sustained by Catholic churches during the war, one would have expected Jujol to
receive important renovation and church-related assignments.
Work did begin to come his way again in 1940, but these commissions, like many projects before the war, were mostly small,
isolated church renovations, limited by the poverty that followed the Catalan defeat. To his great credit, Jujol transformed
many of these interiors, chapels, and altars into beautiful
works, examples of his extraordinary ability to design and produce small environments and architectural collages under dis-
tressed artistic and financial circumstances. Yet these projects

by their decorative nature and scale lack the architectonic base of the early building and renovation projects. Without his prodigious ability to invent with inexpensive, recycled, and commonplace materials these limited projects would have been totally inconsequential. Today they can be seen in the continuum of Jujol's postwar design stretching back to, and extending from, his earlier collagelike architectural works. As a group they deserve independent study free of the bias against interior decoration; but such study is not my intention here. I can only speculate that they were frustrating to an architect who could have anticipated more and larger commissions based on his early accomplishments, frustrating to a degree poignantly in proportion to his patient elaborations of restricted materials in constricted space.

In March 1939 Jujol resumed his position at the technical school. The following year, in May 1940, the School of Architecture reopened and he returned to teaching; there he designed a monument to the school's professors who died on the National, that is, Fascist, anti-Republican side, during the war. After many years of banishment to the school's basement, the memorial tablet with the Falangist insignia has been relocated inconspicuously behind the Càtedra Gaudí. "Every side has its heroes," I was told when shown the stone roster.

Understanding the political situation in Spain, and especially in Catalunya, from the late nineteenth century through the Civil War, is a confusing task. Jujol's life corresponds almost exactly with that tumultuous time. The wounds of the Civil War and Franco's dictatorship are still healing, and to some degree partisan politics from that period are still a factor when interviewing survivors and their children, obscuring full disclosure of events and opinions. By his conservative and religious beliefs Jujol would seem to be automatically aligned with the Nationalists, yet I have seen no evidence of his succumbing to or promoting party politics. What seems clear, and incriminating, if one is looking to align him with the Fascists, is that he was willing to design Nationalist memorials. In addition to the already mentioned memorial tablet, he designed a small monument for Sant Joan Despí.[5] Still, he was effectively inoperative during the war and received no bounty from its victors, unless, of course, the restoration of his teaching positions is considered bounty.[6] Still, Jujol's period of great creativity occurred years before the Civil War.

V

Jujol did little to document his thoughts, his inspiration, or his artistic and political reasoning, which may seem ironic since words—calligraphic texts and symbols—were such an important aspect of his architecture. In many cases, his built works are architectural tablets. He did write one article on each of his Plaça Espanya projects, but neither goes beyond simple descriptions, and their tone is complacent. He was an architect who wrote on buildings and drew with words, but he was not a writer.

His thoughts and critical opinions on his colleagues are basically unknown. While he was working on his commemorative fountain in the Plaça Espanya, only several hundred yards away the 1929 fairground was bursting with construction. He left no record. Pavilions reflecting traditional Spanish architecture were the mainstay, yet several modern pavilions were erected, and under his (and everyone else's) nose Mies van der Rohe inserted one of the seminal works of the twentieth century, The German Pavilion to the International Exhibition, popularly known as the Barcelona Pavilion (re-created on its original site in 1985). Jujol, from the top of his still unfinished fountain at the fair's inauguration would have seen this sleek, spare pavilion intended for the royal inauguration. What might he have thought as he labored at his work—regressive, allegorical, typical—while contemplating the new, so far removed from the *modernisme* with which he began? Again, as with the exhibitions at the Galeries Dalmau, he might have respected, even liked, some aspects of the new: the pavilion would have been problematic for him yet conceivably appreciated on the basis of his own early work with manipulated planes, angles, and light. His recorded thoughts would have provided an important perspective on emerging modernism and the international style, just as they began to claim Barcelona under the banner of the GATEPAC. We are never to know those words and thoughts. Instead we must turn to the hieroglyphics of his built works, his words in stone, steel, and color.

Notes

[1.] David Mackay, *Modern Architecture in Barcelona, 1854-1939* (New York: Rizzoli, 1989).

[2.] The acronym represents the *Grup d'Arquitectes i Tècnics Catalans per al Progrés de l'Arquitectura Contemporània* (Group of Catalan Architects and Technicians for the Progress of Contemporary Architecture).

[3.] GATCPAC was later modified from a Catalan organization to include all of Spain: the first "C," for Catalan, was changed to "E" for Españoles, and the organization became GATEPAC.

[4.] Josep Maria Jujol, Jr., *The Architecture of Josep Maria Jujol,* trans. Ronald Christ (New York: SITES Books, forthcoming).

[5.] Today this stone monument stands neglected. Its dedication and names have all been chipped off, leaving only one innocuous pictorial panel.

[6.] In the politicized atmosphere of postwar Barcelona I do not see how it could be considered otherwise. Surely there is some political unraveling to do here by someone inside Catalunya, someone able to follow what will undoubtedly be a tortuous path.

With Gaudí: Casa Batlló, Casa Milà, & Park Güell

When Republican forces destroyed Gaudí's studio in Sagrada Família during the Civil War, they destroyed not only the bulk of his drawings and documents but also the most likely source of documents on the relationship between Gaudí and Jujol, about which little is known. Not even the exact date or circumstances of Gaudí's hiring Jujol is documented. Their dated projects, the scant and mostly anecdotal testimony of assistants, coworkers, or specialized craftsmen results in little that is trustworthy about their early years together.

Only slightly more is known, and that primarily anecdotal, concerning the mid and late years when Jujol had become Gaudí's trusted associate. By 1906, the nature of the work Gaudí assigned to Jujol indicates the elder architect's confidence in him and attests to Jujol's full integration into the workshop with remarkable artistic independence. At this point Gaudí entrusted Jujol with portions of Casa Batlló's interior and brass hardware, as well as the coloration and design for the ceramic facade, that "huge and insane multicolored mosaic, shimmering with pointillistic iridescence from which the forms of water emerge," as Jujol's fellow Catalan, Dalí, described it.[1]

With Casa Batlló, Gaudí's architecture, enormous and abrupt, changed direction radically. Outdated *renaixença* mass disappeared along with historical quotation and overt allusion as well as the heavy-handed stone work, seen, for example in Palau Güell (1885-89) or Casa Calvet (1898-1904). In their place a light, bonelike system, sheathed by almost inconspicuous undulations of the facade, activated the plane that he more dramatically explored in Casa Milà, then later at Park Güell, and one that Jujol boldly transposed in Casa Planells. Moreover, Gaudí transferred stylistic maneuvers from the renovation of Casa Batlló's facade to its interior: undulating planes, ceramics at once decorative and functional, expressive wrought iron harmonized with a fluid plan.

Questions arise. What caused this change and how was it effected? Some elements at Casa Batlló trace their lineage and pedigree directly to Gaudí's earlier buildings: the metal balcony rails, for example, are closely related in form to those at Casa Calvet, and Casa Batlló's furniture has origins in the pieces from Casa Calvet. Yet this simple and superficial peerage scarcely accounts for such total, complex, and transcendental cohesion of design as Casa Batlló manifests. Could Jujol, just out of architecture school, have influenced and, by his similar artistic disposition but differing talent, thrust Gaudí into his most significant period of design, into one of his signature buildings? In a word, *inspired* him? I think so, agreeing as I do with Carlos Flores's speculation that "although Jujol's collaboration began at a time when Gaudí had already set out on the road to developing new forms of expression, it seems undoubtable that Jujol's personality . . . would have an animating, confirming effect. . . . It is important to emphasize that starting with Casa Calvet and Bellesguard—the last of his historical connections—Gaudí's architecture reveals stylistic variations going beyond a simple development and giving way, in various aspects, to profound changes, genuine ruptures, that irrefutably manifest themselves in Casa Batlló."[2] Further, Flores states that "the presence alongside Gaudí of the young Jujol's reflective, self-possessed temperament, his boundless spontaneity, the lack of inhibition . . . could have served to provoke or at least develop more fully that tapping of the unconscious so clearly detectable in Gaudí during his last phase and in Jujol from the very start."[3]

Following Flores, George Collins came to entertain similar thoughts when he wrote that "we know from Gaudí's sketches for the Casa Calvet chairs of about 1901-02 that he was approximating the [naturalistic, organically inspired] manner himself, but it did not break out until the Casa Batlló with which Jujol was associated."[4] Without devaluing Gaudí's genius, I suggest Jujol as catalyst of Gaudí's transformation. Motivated by the younger architect, Gaudí welcomed, invited Jujol's creative participation (as he did that of other associates attached to his workshop, such as Joan Rubió Belver and Françesc Berenguer). Such was one conduit of Gaudí's genius.

Jujol participated in Gaudí's next projects even more significantly, which may be interpreted as a deepening of the two architects' growing relationship developed through mutual and complementary design objectives. Jujol worked along with Gaudí during the construction of Casa Milà and took charge when Gaudí was away working on his commission at the cathedral in Mallorca. Jujol designed and painted controversial elements for the cathedral that may have led to Gaudí's even-

Antoni Gaudí, Casa Batlló

tual dismissal. In any case, Gaudí remained committed to Jujol's abstract calligraphic work. Casa Milà's contractor, Josep Bayó, noted that the two architects had paralleling points of view, a fact commonly attested but important in this case since as Casa Milà neared completion, Gaudí, after disagreeing with his client, abandoned the work, leaving it to Jujol. Jujol finished the roof ventilators and chimneys, though only one group of small ventilator caps is stylistically distinguishable from the army of others. It, unlike its stuccoed fellows, is decorated with protruding broken glass (a Jujolian device) while the larger chimneys pots are covered with the white, broken ceramic characteristic of Gaudí.

Jujol also contributed to the interiors and designed Casa Milà's balcony rails. Evelyn Waugh saw these grilles and rails on his 1929 taxi tour of Gaudí's work and wrote: "Perhaps the most unexpected thing about this building is the ironwork. . . . Many of the windows have wrought-iron balustrades that are fearless tangles of twisted metal, like the wreckage of an aeroplane that has fallen burning from a great height and has suddenly been cooled by hosings of cold water."[5] In retrospect, we know that the sublime "wreckage" was Jujol's first major design accomplishment, and we appreciate Waugh's choice of *fearless*. Jujol's wrought iron—and here I mean *wrought* in both the artisanal and affective senses—not only complements Gaudí's undulations but also increases our sense of the building as activated. Alone, the master's undulations are tranquil, a calm sea of stone. Jujol's forging brought not only waves and light fractures, it also brought a churning elemental violence that transforms Gaudí's sculpted facade into an architecture of animation. Independently, the twisted interlockings choreograph tractable chaoses of form: linear, abstract Laocoöns. Jujol's design metamorphosizes the railings' functionality.

Here is Jujol's first claim to membership in Europe's avant-garde. And here in these twisted lines of iron is Jujol's entry into a world of abstract, calligraphic, and, subsequently, textual architecture. When we look at photographs or drawings of Casa Milà we can easily see the sketchlike quality of these works of "twisted wreckage"—their calligraphic likeness. His later use of fractured china and glass mosaics, and, even more directly, his further use of wrought iron stem from this seminal detailing of Gaudí's work. These rails portend his future.

Top: Casa Milà
Bottom: Jujol's Casa Milà chimneys

Antoni Gaudí, Casa Milà

18

Never again do we see such calligraphic and sculpturally advanced work from Gaudí. His work never repeats the architectural violence that these storms of metal forge; but we see it continually, in metal, plaster, and paint from Jujol.

What we see on Casa Milà is one of Jujol's masterpieces. His masterpiece burnished into one of Gaudí's. If we think of this overlayering of works as metaphor, extending it to the architects' personalities, we may also deduce violence, not manifested at this date but perhaps approaching after Jujol applies another of his masterworks over one of Gaudí's—on the bench at Park Güell. Just as mystery surrounds the coming together of Gaudí and Jujol, it surrounds their separation. If we follow the argument that Jujol sparked Gaudí into his most creative period and became a trusted collaborator, his sudden departure after producing works unequaled by any other associate of Gaudí's leaves us puzzled. Did work sufficiently interesting for Jujol disappear as Gaudí concentrated on Sagrada Família? Could Gaudí no longer afford him? Did Jujol, realizing his own potential, decide on independence? Or, is it possible that after such individualistic works, peripheral though profound on the surface, Gaudí was singed by jealousy? The answers, unless evidence exists in the private Jujol Archive, probably went up in smoke during the Civil War.

Between Jujol's two masterpieces for Gaudí at Casa Milà and Park Güell, Gaudí assigned him the painting of the Sagrada Família maquette, which Gaudí exhibited to French indifference (if not contempt) at the 1910 Société Nationale des Beaux-Arts in Paris. How much this poor reception in Paris is Jujol's responsibility is unknown, but if Parisians responded to the Sagrada Família maquette the way Church officials responded to Jujol's painting at Mallorca it may be considerable. Regardless of the reception, Gaudí's approval was secure. According to a workshop assistant, the master architect, "seated in an armchair, watched Jujol working. . . . From time to time, Gaudí would repeat devotedly: 'That's good, Jujol, that's good,'"[6] thus reassuring the younger architect of his support. Along the same lines Josep F. Ràfols, himself an assistant to Gaudí, reported that "Gaudí had an absolute faith in Jujol's sense of color."[7] Pieces of the broken maquette did turn up in Gaudí's studio after the Civil War, but they offer little more than a hint of the multicolored vision that Gaudí, via

Antoni Gaudí, Park Güell

20

Jujol, may have had for the nativity facade. (These fragments are now displayed in Sagrada Família's museum.)

The significance of Gaudí's trust, as reflected in this maquette, the facade of Casa Batlló, and the railings at Casa Milà, becomes more apparent in the work he assigned Jujol at Park Güell. There Jujol undertook the design and coloration for the hypostyle's ceiling medallions and, after Gaudí designed the prefabricated concrete bench and gave an outline for its exterior decoration, Jujol carried out and supervised the installation of the botanic, palmlike efflorations along its exterior. For the inside of the bench, however, Jujol was given full responsibility for the design, creating for Gaudí one of his masterpieces.

The coat of many colors for the serpentining bench at Park Güell was Jujol's last major work for Gaudí. In a method used for covering warped surfaces, called *trencadís* (derived from the Catalan verb *trencar*, to break), Jujol recycled cartloads of rejected ceramic as well as the discarded china and glass he and his workmen collected (an architectural version of the discarded cigarette packages or newspapers Picasso and Braque built collages with). Jujol wrought his motley materials into a fractured architectural collage and one of the great abstract and symbolic surfaces in architecture.

Along with this ceramic collage, Gaudí commissioned custom-made capping and backrest tiles on which Jujol drew, scratched, and painted religious texts and signs before having them overglazed and fired. Joan Bassegoda i Nonell, discussing the documentary drawing of these inscriptions by Juan Matamala[8] (an assistant to Gaudí assigned to work under Jujol), has said: "Without question the incisions in the raw clay of the tiles joined helicoidally along the capping portions and backrest of the bench are the work of Josep Maria Jujol."

The inscriptions, monograms, and drawings are among the overlooked aspects of the bench's surface; they are, in fact, its voice. Fragmented, cryptic, and even hidden, their message is carried in a text-collage. Never calling much attention to themselves, these text/tile drawings nevertheless whisper devotional phrases to the Virgin: *son Front* (her brow), *Angelus Domini nuntiavit Maria* ([sic]; the Angel of the Lord spoke unto Mary), *Amb ella via de Pau* (with her the way to peace), and in one case warn the inhabitants of the city to beware of

continued on page 30

Text/Tiles, Park Güell

In a slightly different form, pages 22-29 appeared in SITES Architecture #15, produced in collaboration with Ronald Christ.

The abstracted and often obscure devotions incised into the Park Güell's bench offer one of the most complete views to Jujol's early calligraphy. Here samples of Jujol's writings on, in, and for an architectural surface can be studied for their diverse stylistic variances as well as for his methods of graphic camouflage that he continually refined in almost all his works. Some of the text styles begin to illustrate Jujol's early calligraphic typology; they are paired with Matamala's corresponding 1964 sketches for clarification.

Unique, though typically Jujolian, this vegetal motif on the backrest band of Gaudí's helicoidal tiles is the first incised motif of the series encountered by the visitor when entering the area of the bench. The compositional relationship between the incised motif and the branching lines, leaf designs, and geometric leaflets in the *trencadís* characterizes Jujol's treatment throughout all his work. This particular design-incision is closely related to the fine-line sgraffiti that Jujol used in the transition areas around major sgraffiti designs and a building's stucco facade.

Portions of SITES's working video script correspond to the shaded area the map. The Catalan words *son front* (her brow), appear in somewhat simplified or regularized form in Matamala's drawings (Jujol's barb on the cross bar, like the descending swash at the bottom of the "t", are missing, while the principal curves in the "s" have been exaggeratedly thickened), as is evident from comparison with the photograph below.

Clearly lettered—even more clearly represented by
Matamala—this inscription may puzzle the viewer by its
placement on the backrest, its contracted Catalan, its
somewhat cryptic meaning. Expressing his extremely
personal devotion to the Virgin in colloquial Catalan—*tum
serveixes* rather than *tu em servixes*—Jujol identified the
Virgin as serving him. In contrast to the curving roundness
of *son front*, these joined letters do not flow or run; rather,
they angulate sharply, more in the style of early
Phoenician or Greek letters.

angelus Domini nuntiavit Maria

A symbolically blue tile on the backrest repeats the biblical annunciation in Jujol's idiosyncratic Latin: *angelus Domini nuntiavit Maria*. Varying strokes of half-uncial and rounded lettering with angular lines like those in Phoenician or ancient Greek alphabets (compare the square "n" in *angelus* with the rounded "m" and "n" of *Domini*), Jujol disintegrated some letters and introduced a kind of calligraphic abstraction, minimized by Matamala, who apparently intended to render legible what many still find difficult to decipher. The wash of blue overglaze across the entire inscription both masks the message and integrates it into a graphic as well as religious meaning: blue is traditionally associated with the Virgin.

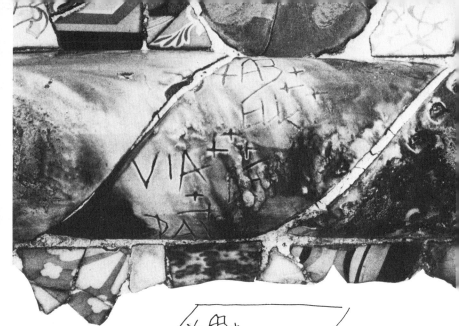

Ligatures creating diphthongs—as in the "b" of this tile's first word, which, by being drawn against the initial "a," simulta-

neously serves as the word's central "m," upended—abound in the bench. A comparable ligature in the next word, links the final "a" of *ella*, to the preceding double "ll," now made to resemble an inverted monogram for the Virgin. So beguiling are these "characteristic calligraphic games of Jujol," as Carlos Flores calls them, that Matamala mistook the fourth word, *de*, in this motto which occurs several times in the bench: *AMB ELLA VIA DE PAU* (WITH HER THE WAY TO PEACE). Such a way, for Jujol, nec-essarily was the way of the cross and of the stars, which he combined in stylized forms that relate to designs elsewhere in the bench.

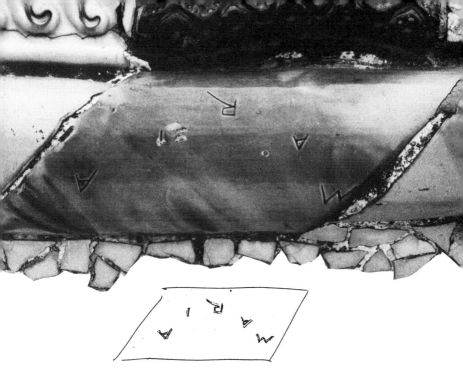

The inverted arc Jujol devised for the Virgin Mary's name answers the "found" arc of the section of molding tile he place above it—the manufactured elaborateness of the one decorating the handcrafted, Roman simplicity of the other. In this detail, the shifting relationship of part to part and part to whole embodies the method and effects of Jujol's entire composition.

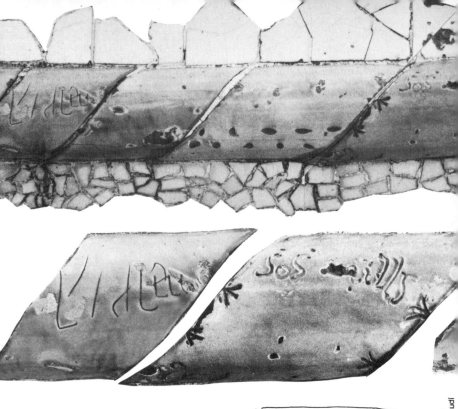

Matamala's drawings
courtesy: Catedra Gaudi

Four styles of calligraphy in this portion of the backrest represent, from left to right, MARIA (upside down), *ay! sos ulls* (oh! her eyes), *tota esglesia* (upside down; whole church), and a monogram "M" encircled by a crown. The range from seemingly hastily scratched lines for the first word (far left), which Matamala represents with double shadowed lines rather than the single strokes of the original, to the sinuously curling, *modernisme* impression of the monogram (far right), which Matamala's sketch accurately reveals as being made of discrete, overlapping elements, displays but does not exhaust Jujol's calligraphic vocabulary in the bench. While Jujol typically subtracted elements in the almost disintegrated name of MARIA (no descender, in the Greek manner, on the "R," or linking to the stem on the second "a"), he elaborately extended, combined, and added symbolically decorative elements to the letters of *tota esglesia* (upside down and written without its accent on the second "e") so that some are nearly illegible (the initial "e" lying on its back, twining horizontally to link with the haloed, slender "s" whose curves are squeezed into a near vertical that skips the adjacent "g" to descend into an "e" like the first but upright this time). Characteristically, Jujol man-

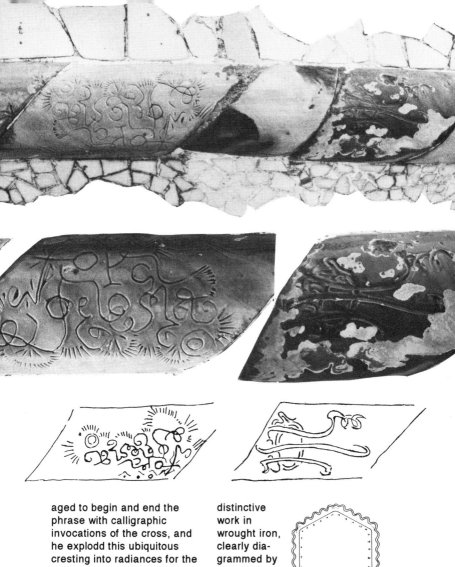

aged to begin and end the phrase with calligraphic invocations of the cross, and he explodd this ubiquitous cresting into radiances for the entire phrase. Even with a stylized band of heavenly bodies above and the concentric sun on the left, the tile's religious iconography simultaneously predicts the playful arabesques of Miró's painting. In contrast, the *sos ulls* tile, whose *ay!* in the lower left corner Matamala ignored, offers the simple, discontinuous elements of Jujol's noncursive rounded script; while the horizontal monogram, especially in its crown (left of tile), recalls Jujol's

distinctive work in wrought iron, clearly diagrammed by Matamala. Each separate tile has elements of the others in it, and they are all unified as a composition by intervening elements, including the nearly parallel bands of indented brown seed shapes pointing toward the cresting of the *sos ulls* tile, which in turn predict the radiating lines on *tota esglesia*, whose yellowish background flows between the next tile's darker boundaries, which overglaze the monogram.

continued from page 21

their wicked ways. The varying calligraphic styles—san-serif, cursive, and *modernisme*—further diminish immediate, overall recognition. There is even a style like Miró's drawings, and Miró's greater fame does not alter the fact that he knew Park Güell, so perhaps we should say that Miró's line is Jujolian. Even *Time Magazine* acknowledged this lineage in its review of the Miró exhibition at the Museum of Modern Art written by Robert Hughes. Hughes stated: "The mosaic inventions of the Catalan artist Josep Maria Jujol, who worked for Gaudí when Miró was a teenager, and whose wandering line and isolated words in tile clearly stayed in Miró's mind as he did his poem-pictures."[9]

In addition to the colloquial Catalan and idiosyncratic Latin phrases that the seventy-four-year-old Matamala recorded in 1967, Ronald Christ and I photographed and mapped the bench's surface in 1984, identifying several that he overlooked and verifying that some have disappeared.[10] The missing inscriptions may 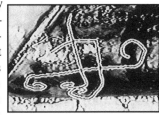 have disappeared through vandalism, weather damage, or inappropriate and indifferent maintenance and numerous "renovations." Carlos Flores identifies two inscriptions as Jujol's monogram: one, an incised "J" cut through with a cross-stroke combines Jujol's initial and the symbol of the crucifixion; the other, the letter "t" in the phrase *son front*, represents a stylized cross as well as the initial "J." While documenting all these inscriptions, I discovered a previously undocumented monogram that is much more typical of the monogram Jujol used to sign his drawings. After onsite inspection, Jujol, Jr., positively identified it as his father's signature. Under heavy glaze and on the underside of the backrest, Jujol incised double "J"s with a cross-bar curling in opposite directions at each end. Jujol literally and repeatedly inscribed himself in his work.

UNESCO has named Park Güell to its register of international patrimony, and funds for its preservation have allowed important restoration and preservation work to proceed, including work on the bench's beautiful and volatile tiles. Some extant, legible tiles are beyond recognition; others beyond restoration. Those that exist continue to provide a glori-

Jujol's monogram on the bench at Park Güell, computer enhanced

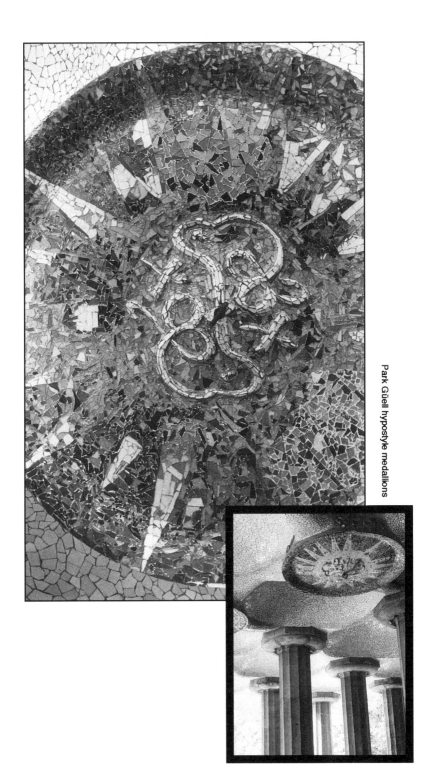

Park Güell hypostyle medallions

ous face and voice in *trencadís* for the bench's architectural surface, as well as a surface for the architectural form.

Below the bench, in the so-called Hall of the Hypostyles, Gaudí left the sites of two Doric columns empty in order to provide open areas in what he intended to serve as a market space. Jujol then created *trencadís* medallions to fill the circular voids where the columns would have engaged the ceiling. His materials included tiles, dinner china, portions of bottles, mirrors, and even a porcelain doll. These large medallions and their orbiting smaller ones (fourteen in all), are direct ancestors of modern collage and predate cubist works. Through Jujol's compositional ordering, they affirm the beauty of common materials and proclaim an artistic vitality for materials considered trash—random bits of glazed or vitreous chromatic information bonded together to create a unit of artistic expression.

Gaudí had experimented with mosaic, or *trencadís*, at least as early as 1887 at Finca Güell and 1889 for the chimneys of Palau Güell, though not until Casa Batlló and Jujol's presence did he employ it as a primary architectural surface, rather than as isolated units or random decorations. At Park Güell, Jujol fully realized the method's architectural, textual, and abstract artistic possibilities in the ceiling medallions; on the outside of the bench, where Gaudí had requested that the designs function like acroteria to complement his Doric hypostyle below; and finally on the inside of the bench, where Jujol brought *trencadís* to full maturity, integrating both the religious phrases, abstraction, planned patterning, and, in a few instances, full pictorial ceramic items (for example, a soup plate from his family's dinner service). Jujol basically confined his use of *trencadís* to that portion of the bench between the custom-made backrest and the capping tiles, making only occasional mosaic forays onto or below the seat, where the remainder of the ceramic surfacing is white and similar to the tile on the roof of Casa Milà. Gaudí's work never broadly displays *trencadís* after Park Güell. It was Jujol's to reemploy at Can Negre, Can Bofarull, and especially Torre de la Creu, the latter begun in 1913, the same year he may have completed the bench.

Acknowledging that some of Gaudí's most loved and respected architectural elements came from a Gaudí-Jujol collaboration and in some cases directly from the mind and hands of Jujol, and after presenting contemporary and historic testimony of Jujol's importance in the master's studio, I want to echo Carlos Flores: "Once the dialectical process underlying the relationship between Gaudí and Jujol has been considered from the perspective of disciple to master, it is time to measure how many as well as how essential and irreplaceable were the influences that flowed in the opposite direction, that is, from master to disciple. Summing up the phenomenon pointedly and briefly, one might say *the example of Gaudí is ever present in Jujol's work.*"[10] Thus we can look to Jujol as an independent architect even while tracking Gaudí's "ever present" influences. And, even as we see aspects of Gaudí's permeation of Jujol, we will see how Jujol's genius for detail, so brilliantly exploited on Gaudí's structures—specifically the cast iron of Casa Milà and the ceramic and text at Park Güell—prepared for and advanced his own architecture.

Spanish stamp with Gaudí and Casa Milà

Notes

1. Quoted in R. Descharnes and C. Prevost, *Gaudí the Visionary* (New York: Viking Press, 1982), 158.

2. Carlos Flores, SITES 11, *An Introduction and Guide to the Architecture of Jujol* (New York: Lumen, Inc., 1983), 20-21.

3. Ibid, 24.

4. George Collins, SITES 11, *An Introduction and Guide to the Architecture of Jujol* (New York: Lumen, Inc., 1983), 15.

5. Evelyn Waugh, SITES 15, *Gaudí*, reprinted and annotated from the *Architectural Review*, June 1930 (New York: Lumen, Inc., 1986), 7.

6. Jujol, Jr., *The Architecture of Josep Maria Jujol.*

7. Josep F. Rafòls, *La arquitectura de J. Ma. Jujol* (Barcelona: Col.legi d'Arquitectes de Catalunya, 1974).

8. Matamala's sketch-survey is preserved in the Càtedra Gaudí.

9. Robert Hughes, *Time Magazine*, "The Purest Dreamer" (New York, November 8, 1993) 46.

10. This survey of every backband and capping tile on the bench resulted in a 24-foot photographic map. It was produced in conjunction with the SITES videotape *Text/Tiles, Jujol/Gaudí, Bench/Park Güell*, by Dennis Dollens and Ronald Christ. Portions appeared in SITES 15, 1986, 16-23.

11. Flores, SITES 11, 25.

Jujol's sketch, Casa Mañach

Jujol Archive

Drawings, Casa Mañach chair

D. DOLLENS

34

Casa Mañach

Among a number of small projects Jujol independently designed while still working with Gaudí, one, a small retail store,
illustrates strategies of design he would return to or continuously develop for the rest of his life and thus deserves viewing as an important antecedent to his later architecture. Commissioned by Peré Mañach, an industrialist, arts patron, and
one of Picasso's early supporters, Casa Mañach was begun by
Jujol in 1911. It was his first important, independently designed
work to be built, and he crafted *modernisme* forms, graphics,
and calligraphy into the signage. He also merged them with,
and to a large extent used them to define, the interior and exterior design, thereby transforming the established, wisping
lines of *modernisme* into an expressionist work. This is the first
time we see Jujol's transformation of calligraphy into architectonic elements—a deployment that will become more important and more fully controlled in his next projects.

     According to Jujol, Jr., Mañach had become interested
in Gaudí's work and became friends with the architect. Although there is no record of Mañach asking Gaudí to design his
store, this is possible since it was Gaudí who Mañach admired.
Perhaps Gaudí in turn introduced Mañach to Jujol with the intention of steering the job toward the young architect. Since the
elder architect had withdrawn from secular commissions and
because the renovation offered work of a limited scale, such a
sequence is probable.

     Casa Mañach disappeared years ago, so
we must look to the surviving descriptions,
sketches, and photographs for hints of its design
presence and the way it relates to Jujol's later
work. However a few pieces of its furniture have
survived and from them we may induce Jujol's
spatial and decorative inten-
tions.

     The contemporary
photographs of Casa Mañach
offer evocative clues to the
architect's later works, design
process, and aesthetic intentions. But studying the furni-

ture, especially the chairs, more concretely, we can see that in these 1911 experiments with form and space Jujol had moved further and in even more radical directions with furniture than Gaudí had. Perhaps Jujol was influenced by Gaudí's furniture for Casa Calvet or Casa Batlló; possibly Jujol was instrumental in Gaudí's designs. In any case, neither the furniture for Casa Calvet and Casa Batlló, nor the pews for Colonia Güell manage to suggest the dynamic movement or the spatial sophistication realized in Jujol's small metal and wood chairs.

Like Gaudí's chairs, the Mañach chairs are iconic. Their sculptural qualities prompt scrutiny before their form suggests rest. They require consideration as objects distinct from traditional chairs even as they attend to the task of seating. With these fixtures Jujol turned topsy-turvy Le Corbusier's dictum "a chair is in no way a work of art; a chair has no soul; it is a machine for sitting in." With these chairs Jujol created functional sculpture or sculptural furniture in a syntax of fluid space.

The components of the metal frame are joint-welded, hand forged, and hammered nearly round in section (if the iron bars began round they were hammered irregular). At close range, flat spots in the frame show facetlike, continually breaking and refracting light. These facets thwart the appearance of regularity or any perception of symmetry in the structural components, just as the assembled frame falsifies any spatial regularity. Taken as a unit, the chair interrupts traditional modulated space and reorders it polymorphically, leaving the impression of perpetual flux within the chair's structural confines. This smithwork is closely related in effect to the architectural iron work Jujol created for Casa Milà and to what he would later create in rails and fences for his own projects. Closely following the completion of Casa Milà's balcony rails the chairs demonstrate some of the same concerns—experimental use of material, fragmented space, and broken and patterned light—and these concerns remain dominant in the architect's work for the rest of his life. If inspected as architectural models as well as experiments in form, these chairs can be seen as conceptual armatures from which Jujol later realized his most important building, the church at Vistabella.

The experience of viewing one of these chairs is unsettling: they seem imbued with movement, evolving in space,

Jujol's abstract serrated key in Casa Mañach logo

Interior, Casa Mañach

37

revealing a nonspecific organic unit that seems to change from each angle of vision. In sculpture, a parallel may be drawn between Umberto Boccioni's *Unique Forms of Continuity in Space* (1913). Both sculpture and chair conjure a state of aerodynamic flutter, while both intimate propulsion. Inanimate objects, they look as if they are about to hurl themselves into space—linearly forward for Boccioni, helicoidally around and up for Jujol.

Jujol mobilized, stirred the space immediately around and within the confines of the chair to act in conjunction with the fluid, hammered metal, making a metal cage described by sine curves. This frame rests on flat, hammered-metal paws, then rises as a tripod: the front leg to the seat; the rear left directly to the backrest, with a small appendage reaching out to brace the seat; the rear right leg, doing just the opposite: reaching directly to the seat with a welded appendage branching up to support the backrest.

Looking selectively at the chair's front elevation suggests the possibility of a calibrated, triangulated system behind the design; even the wooden, heart-shaped seat and back may be inscribed easily within a triangle. But other elevations belie this categorization. From these profiles, the downward and curved trajectory of the legs bound by a metallic serpentine lasso, reveals the triangular and triangularlike shapes and components as elements within a conceptual form probably arrived at abstractly, intuitively, perhaps symbolically.

Only two Mañach chairs are extant, each slightly different from the other, though they are faithful to one another's principal form. They, along with the surviving table, evidence Jujol's break with Catalan turn-of-the-century spatial relations. Their form displays some of the plastic frontiers scouted by the thirty-two-year-old architect. Their overall sculptural effect denies rational space and traditional building systems while still providing Jujol with a vehicle for religious symbolism. In this case, he took a symbol for the suffering of both Christ and Mary Immaculate, the heart, as a major design element for the chair's seats and backs and modified it by curving the tip to the left as he had seen it at the Cathedral of Tarragona, where it appears on the 1666 cloister tombstone of

1666 Tombstone detail

Facade and interior, Casa Mañach

Hyacinit i Brava.[1]

    Jujol, Jr.'s account attests to the minor sensation in Barcelona when Casa Mañach was completed: unconventional and early use of electrical illumination, as well as the expressionistic signage brought people out of their way to see for themselves what we can only glimpse in obscured photographs. Judged from the pictures, the story seems plausible and is further born out by John Richardson in his biography of Picasso: "The showroom that he [Mañach] commissioned Josep Maria

Jujol to design on the Carrer Ferran (now destroyed) in 1911 boasted decoration that was far more advanced than anything in Paris, Vienna or London. Jujol . . . frescoed the ceilings and walls of the principal gallery with freeform arabesques, curlicues and polka dots, which predict Miró's work of the thirties."[2] Jujol created a modern work as daring as any sets seen in German expressionist films (*The Cabinet of Dr. Caligari* was shot eight years later), and there is every likelihood that it would have been a sensational destination for a population accustomed to urban observations on their *paseos*.

The facade, in its geometric partitioning, chamfered display window, and graphic decoration was Jujol's first mature architectural work. The use of graphics to subvert ordinary architectural junctures and perspective, the merging of calligraphy into architectural planes, and the employment of covert devotional iconography—specifically the letter "M" (Mañach/Maria) for the door plate—integrated for the first time modes of design Jujol would incorporate even more fully in future projects.

• • •

Similar to the chair's mobilized space is the spatial sculpting of an elevator Jujol designed in 1913 for an apartment building on Carrer Mallorca in Barcelona. Unlike the chair's metaphorical acceleration, the elevator actually lifts into space, splitting the design into two compatible but independent units, a protective cage and an elevator carriage. The cage, a simple, curved form of open-wire metal mesh, surrounds the carriage when stationary and protects its landing pad during lift-off. The upper edge of this fencelike cage is banded with serpentining metal ribbon that suggests the origins of Torre de la Creu's fence or recalls the undulations of Casa Milà and the Park Güell bench. In Jujol's typology of forms it can be seen as an early representative of forged and bent iron sculpturally related to other of his rails, gates, and banisters.

The carriage is finely crafted of polished wood, brass, glass, and mirror, and is distinctive, with its open undulating roof and its curved, beveled glass window. From the inside, these two forms, along with the reflections from interior mirrors, perceptually fracture and recombine the lobby interior,

Elevator, Carrer Mallorca

Jujol's elevator sketches

Jujol Archive

manipulating views as well as the ordinary experience of
mechanized vertical movement in slow moving, semi-open vertical ascent and descent.

Notes

[1] It is worth recalling that, while venerable in its history, the devotion to the Sacred Heart of Christ was introduced into the Church
calendar so late as 1856 by Pius IX. The beatification in 1864 of
Margaret Mary Alacoque, a seventeenth-century petitioner for the cult,
greatly renewed its fervor, with special impetus in Catalunya, so the
synechdochical heart in Jujol's works reflects a Catalan Catholicism
of broader scope than Jujol's personal symbolism.

[2] John Richardson, *A Life of Picasso*, Volume 1: 1881-1906 (London:
Pimlico, 1992), 164.

Torre de la Creu

I no longer believe it possible to find another contemporary European building more spatially and stylistically experimental than Torre de la Creu. Yet, when completed in Sant Joan Despí, a small town outside Barcelona, it stood not only provincially isolated but intellectually unrecognized — much as it stands today. Jujol never participated in the avant-garde; he built without the hyperbole of manifestos or publicity.

This unsung monument, only twenty-minutes by train from Barcelona's Plaça Catalunya, is one of the handful of projects that comprises the scattered museum of Jujol's work, the fragmented and fragmentary embodiment of his architectural craft and vision, otherwise known as Sant Joan Despí. After Torre de la Creu and Can Negre, most of Jujol's work here memorializes a downward spiral in his architectural practice, manifest in the increasingly modest, even inconsequential projects the architect was obliged to undertake because they were all that came to him. The causes of this promise-shattering decline elude strict categorization, based as they are in reciprocating forces of general culture and specific biography. Among them, however, I speculate on two: a possible overshadowing by Gaudí, in whose light Jujol first came to view and against whose blaze he may have seemed an epigone; and the counter-effect of his orthodox Catholicism and its consequent conservatism. The very "Franciscanism" that robes our image of the later Gaudí and emanated no less powerfully, through far less ostentatiously, from Jujol may have alienated him — financially as well as politically — from those in a position to commission him. His notorious virtue may have been a fault at this point in Catalunya's changing social scene. By the mid-1920s, the political and social atmosphere in Catalunya was one of worker's egalitarianism; and, even if the Church was a primary source of inspiration for Jujol, to the man on the street it was also a primary source of workers' repression, an institution

Torre de la Creu nearing completion

Postcard view, Setmana Tràgica

42

allied with the factory and landowners, and later with the Fascists. We need only remember the riotous events of Setmana Tràgica (Tragic Week) in 1909 and the looting and burning of twenty-two churches and thirty-four convents to consider just how pervasive anti-Church sentiment was.

The small city of Sant Joan Despí, annexed to Barcelona by urban growth, inadvertently became a laboratory for Jujol. For nearly thirty-six years, starting with Torre de la Creu, through his 1929 appointment as the city's auxiliary municipal architect to his death in 1949, Jujol built, planned, and decorated here. Compact and simple in plan, the city's core, even though spotted with shoddy modern apartment buildings violating its nineteenth- and early twentieth-century scale, would still be recognized by Jujol.

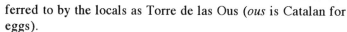

Jujol Archive

Stepping off the train from Barcelona, just as Jujol did thousands of times, you are faced, across the tracks, by Torre de la Creu's cylinders and mosaic domes, their multilevel undulations making a sky-bound knoll of gleaming ceramic partially obscured by tall eucalyptus trees. This auspicious location gives the building the literal status of architectural landmark, and early on it became a popular one as well. Because its domes resemble a cluster of cupped eggs, the house was and sometimes still is re-

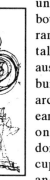

Torre de la Creu under construction

ferred to by the locals as Torre de las Ous (*ous* is Catalan for eggs).

Torre de la Creu, early plan and sketch

Manfredo Tafuri and Francesco Del Co noted that "Jujol surrealistically deformed hallucinated geometries in a pleasing encounter between solidly structured plans and jagged forms."[1] Their general observation is an apt vantage point from which Torre de la Creu may be considered. Jujol designed the structure as a two-family unit. In plan, three primary circles de-

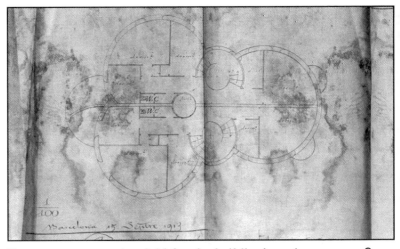

Original ground floor plan on linen

lineate an errant epicycloid for the building's main rooms, while three smaller circles mark service spaces for the entrance and stairways in a clear hierarchy of served and serving. These six intersecting circles rise as intersecting cylinders — similar in massing and elevation to those iconic images in the development of European modernism: grain elevators.[2] Did Jujol happen onto such a combination, perhaps playing with a vocabulary of standard geometric forms that included an epicycloid of three cusps? The game would have been to see which of the forms generated valuable intersecting volumes when raised in elevation. Such play would develop naturally as a result of architecture school, and we know that the plot for Torre de la Creu fulfilled an aunt's promise of a graduation gift. Ludic or not, the plan emphasizes precisely that: planning, and it denotes a pole contrary to the improvisatory makeshift for which Jujol acquired such a reputation and of which Can Negre provides the example. Or was Jujol stimulated by a supra-personal spirit that later impelled Le Corbusier and Mendelsohn? We can't know, of course, but we can now recognize that Torre de la Creu was prophetic and that had it been published and circulated, it might have affected the dialogue of practical and theoretical modernism. Even though Torre de la Creu predates *Vers une Architecture* by ten years, Le Corbusier's dictum seems induced from Jujol's example: "Mass and surface are determined by the plan. The plan is the generator." Once we accept that this basic tenet of modernism found such precocious

Torre de la Creu

expression in the isolation of a small Catalan town we may be on our way to accepting the need to revise architectural history—modernism's as well as Jujol's.

Torre de la Creu's plan is a potent generator, its circular layout generating its architectural form, as well as its symbolism. Three primary cylinders rise to covering parabolic domes; smaller cylinders, sprouting higher, one above the other, are capped with flared domes resting on posts, while the stumpy, semiround portico terminates at the second floor. The lower of the three major towers is symbolically dedicated to Saint Josep, patron saint of the owner; the higher tower to the Virgin Mary. Could this be Jujol's secular, mimetic Sagrada Família? Functionally, the narrow cylinders house circular stairs, effectively creating tubes for vertical circulation. From the ground floor one can spiral up the stairs to the mosaic surfaced roof and emerge, sheltered, under a flared dome, in a mirador. For this ceramic-clad roof Jujol designed and interconnected a series of "hallucinated geometries": stairs, paths, observation posts, rails, and seats that transform the roof into a small, almost surrealistic, ceramic park that is sculpturally far more complex than his mentor's vast work at Park Güell, and more compact and spatially intricate than the expansive roof of Casa Milà or Palau Güell, from which Jujol's initial inspiration may have derived.

Two parabolic arches in the semicircular portico indicate the original, separate entries to the apartments. In an insensitive renovation, the two doorways behind the arches were replaced by one and the dividing wall separating them removed. The original interior was also bisected, separating the two living units. This spatial caesura and Jujol's counterpoint right-angle partitions create a merger between working, dynamic form and spatial violence—an architectural chaos—that is consistent in all his major work. Torre de la Creu illustrates Jujol's response to direction, movement, and encased spaces with a confrontation of opposites: the orthogonal cutting the circular, flowing forms violated straight walls and right angles. Responding to this binary counterpoint of form, David Mackay noted in *Modern Architecture in Barcelona* that Jujol's manipulation of space and forms to meet their opposites "is an original characteristic that sets Jujol's work apart from, and to some extent above, that of Gaudí."[3] For Jujol, intersecting ar-

Jujol Archive

Left: Stairway landing
Top: Stairway detail

chitectural geometries created conjunctures not only of their architectural form but of the almost baroque spaces they tangibly encapsulated. The juncture of form was where he celebrated or obscured the boundaries of architecture, working diverse materials and construction methods into tectonic harmony in order to exploit space.

At Torre de la Creu the two narrow cylinders not only wrap stairways and introduce natural illumination, they also provide the point where the house's symbolic and functional directive, up and down, is manifested for daily usage. The stairways are transformed from the merely functional to the equivalent of directional sign: the spiral stair becomes the information channel for people moving between rooms. The stairs literally screw the building's spaces together. What in traditional domestic architecture is horizontal hallway or gallery is here vertical, helicoidal tubes, twisting and cutting through domestic space. And at the main-floor landing Jujol created a juncture where the practical lacing together of spaces is transformed into an elegant and sweeping conjuncture of material, form, and space. This flowing of stairway into ground floor moves far beyond what could be expected in such restricted space. Either flowing down or leading up, the collision of circular form, splaying steps, twisted and gold-leafed metal, polished wood, and, overhead, calligraphic plaster inscriptions cloud the interiors in a frozen architectural tornado.

Other parts of the interior's detailing are now lost, renovation having merged the two units into one, resulting in large, curvilinear ground-floor spaces instead of the original, orthographic divisions. But some fragments do remain: decorative plasterwork, beautiful metal stair rails that coil upward like intertwined ribbons, and a series of cast-iron columns that support the openings for curving bay windows at the rear of the building, where a single open room has replaced the units' side-by-side dining rooms. In this opened area, the slender columns rise to abstract, gnarly capitals that seem strapped to the shaft with a downward-leading metallic band.

Two floors up, the interior spaces of the bedrooms open to the inside domes of their sheltering, ovoid forms. These bedrooms, like the vaulted space we will see at Vistabella, are among Jujol's most decoratively unencumbered and free spaces. Jujol allows them to simply reflect the inside of his exterior form—interiors sculpted by exterior structure. With a seamless transition from vertical walls to domed ceiling, the rooms take on a likeness to a white planetarium or, for those with a more domestic imagination, the inside of a gigantic half eggshell capping a cylinder of the same circumference.

Exterior modifications have not altered the structure's massing, though most were unnecessary and counter the spirit of Jujol's original. The original wooden-framed windows of both stairway cylinders have been filled in with glass block that from some angles mistakenly give the house a 1930s air. Probably the most deceiving, because the most notable, aspect of the renovation is the ceramic roof work. The deteriorated original required replacing, and the architect's daughter, Tecla, designed a mosaic restoration, we are told, "in the spirit of the original." Since detailed photographs have not yet come to light, we can only speculate that Jujol's original pattern would have been even more abstract and symbolic, in the manner of the Park Güell bench he had recently completed or of his later tower roof at Can Bofarull. Still, I want to stress that these renovations were executed at a time when few people in Catalunya were paying attention to the preservation of *modernisme* buildings and even fewer to Jujol's work.

Torre de la Creu is one of Jujol's few freestanding

Wrought iron gate and detail

buildings and his first important commission not based on renovation. The nature of the overlapping cylinders makes it a three-dimensional structure as interesting to see from one point or angle as from any other; still it yields differences at every view. The building's cylinders might seem to have grown out of the earth in the small garden site and Jujol fronted them with some of his finest work in iron—a simple, slightly undulating fence crenelated with jagged and spiked wrought iron that looks as if it had been torn and twisted with superhuman strength. For its gate, Jujol directed his craftsman to forge the hinges and lock plate into abstract vegetal forms, thereby linking—literally forging a link between—the garden surrounding the house and the barrier to the site. The fence's overall effect closely relates to the craftsmanship and resultant tortured forms of the balcony rails Jujol designed for Casa Milà, though the fence does not transcend his earlier accomplishment. It is an up-close object, hence detailed; the railings are far-off objects, hence bigger generalizations: the contrasting scale of one work to the other is visual as well as spatial and, as a result, the Casa Milà rails are, by definition and effect, greater. The successful transcription in scale is one measure of Jujol's abilities; the

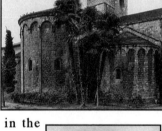

rare accomplishment at such scale in Casa Milà is one measure of what his fate prevented him from accomplishing.

Torre de la Creu's towers and flared domes recall the silhouettes of Islamic forms; perhaps minarets were a historic source. More likely, though, Jujol found his inspiration much closer to

home, not in Islamic elevations, but in the fortresslike cylinders of Romanesque churches that dot Catalunya. From childhood he knew monuments like the Church of the Miracle in his native city, Tarragona; and early in his life he walked and explored the countryside, often with some architectural ruin, sanctuary, or monument as a goal. Considering his reliance on Christian symbolism and his appreciation of local traditions and forms, it seems altogether possible that he found sources for Torre de la Creu in structures like the eleventh-century cylindrical church at Cervera, Sant Pere Gros; in the intersecting

Top: Sant Pau
Bottom: Cevera

50

Torre de la Creu, garden view

51

cylindrical apses of Sant Serni de Tavernoles, or those of small Romanesque chapels like Sant Pau in Barcelona.

Jujol applied overt religious symbolism—prayers, invocations, and  emblems—to nearly all his projects, and Torre de la Creu was no exception: in a single graphic unit two "Ave"s abut the exterior monogram of the Virgin on the portico and effectively claim the building, establishing the text and symbol much as an escutcheon does on many other houses. Inside, undulating above the stairway, Jujol wrote *Déu hi sia* (May God Dwell Here) in waving and cresting plaster. And, if we can rely on the ceramic cladding of the renovation, the various roofs are inscribed in calligraphic monograms and symbols that evolve heavenward. The lowest ceramic levels are decorated with earth and vegetal colors; mid-level the ceramic depicts blue wave forms; and the upper level can be read as fire, with its highest point topped by a wrought-iron cross whose cut and twisted edge etherializes the solid form into aspirational flames—an evolution through earth, water, and fire to God. The name of the house—its logos—thus finds its course and fulfillment in the pedestal building and eponymous finial.

We see in these brief texts and symbols, prefigured in the bench at Park Güell, how Jujol traced his faith in, on, and through his architecture; how words and phrases became a part of the architectural surface, as important as any other building layer, element, or material. These texts lead us to architecture as tablet and warn us that Jujol was not solely concentrating on abstraction and decoration, that semiotic references, bold and furtive, are an integral part of his architecture of devotion.

The precise structural influences on this grouping of joined cylinders remains a mystery. Who knows if he ever considered or appreciated his work in a European context? We, however, can recognize that Torre de la Creu is contemporary with Rudolf Steiner's Dornach projects, though more fully resolved in terms of plan and circular and cylindrical resolution; that it predates Bruno Taut's expressionist Glass Pavilion at the 1914 Werkbund Exhibition as well as Eric Mendelsohn's 1917-21 Einstein Tower; and that it anticipates, by more than fourteen years, Konstantin Melnikov's Moscow house.

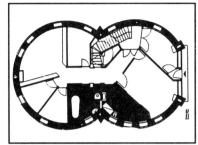

What is more, Melnikov's design, though better known, is timid when compared to Jujol's. The two intersecting cylinders of the Moscow house, its single stair, and roof terrace are functionally close to Jujol's but less geometrically fluid, failing to generate as dynamic an elevation or plan as Torre de la Creu. That Melnikov knew Jujol's work is unlikely and not to the point. What matters is that we now consider Jujol in a broader European context, including Melnikov's. Compared with the work of Melnikov, Taut, and Mendelsohn, Torre de la Creu places in the same front rank of European modernism and deserves corresponding recognition.

More than any other works by Jujol, Torre de la Creu and the earlier and now phantom Casa Mañach approximate mainstream expressionism. His other designs merge styles so thoroughly that grouping them becomes problematic, leaving each to an individual category within Jujol's own hybridized vocabulary.

Plan and main facade, Melnikov's house, 1927

Notes
[1] Manfredo Tafuri and Francesco Dal Co, *Modern Architecture*, vol.1, trans. Robert Erich Wolf (New York: Rizzoli, 1986), 79.
[2] Usually the house is said to be comprised of five cylinders but this leaves the one-storied portico/entry unaccounted for.
[3] Mackay, *Modern Architecture in Barcelona,* 87.

Can Negre

Hybridization is nowhere more apparent than at Can Negre, only a few short blocks from Torre de la Creu. Jujol began this masterwork in 1915, two years after Torre de la Creu, and he worked on it for the next fifteen years. Like many of his commissions to come, it was an expansion and renovation, in this case of a traditional 1680 farmhouse. Small and rectangular in plan and elevation, Jujol caused Can Negre to occupy a design world in and of itself.

54

Jujol Archive

Like Torre de la Creu, Can Negre aspires; yet unlike its nearby relative it does so in a planar way, more as a facade-tablet, a vehicle for text and calligraphic design. Can Negre comprises basic planes meeting at right angles, its front and rear facades dynamically overlaid with drawn vegetation and text. Can Negre's facade calmly undulates its way skyward as it defies what would otherwise be a planar rectangle. But, in a roll of architectural forms, its carriagelike *tribuna* and windows extrude horizontally, showing the facade not only as a vertical tablet but also as a building with horizontal interests of served and serving spaces.

This undulating and rolling house was renovated by Jujol with traditional building materials sympathetic to its original wood, straw, plaster, glass, concrete, and wrought iron. But even so, the renovation preys on its host, nearly engulfing the antique building, living off it while living on it. Jujol took the original farm structure as his core, added rooms to each side, raised a new roof, and cloistered all behind retablelike front and rear facades.

Can Negre
Garden pergola

57

Can Negre is not only parasitical on the 1690 structure but on anyone trying to read it—it feeds off of one's experiences, forcing one to decode, give meaning to, or turn away from it. It requires active reading to find, link, and unlock its text and symbols. You ignore it or you read and work it. Its forms are made complex with surfaces of painted and scratched graphics and religious text. Can Negre's design conspires to include the viewer in its narrative, transforming gaze into reading.

In a sweeping glance, one might group this house within a number of contemporary movements. But when explored, it reveals Jujol's religious and symbolic vision and becomes a work that eludes simple categorization. In, on, and through it Jujol painted and incised decorative and religious images. A hierophant, he attempted to catechize the residents' imagination and past spiritual experience via his own, creating a bond of interpretation—rather like that in ecclesiastical buildings—with the user by employing shared symbols, to make of it an architectural missal that provides the logos of the building and life. The house is a drawn and sculpted vision, where line is metaphor leading to myth and mystery, in order to support faith.

Sitting in a small plaza, which corresponds to the boundaries of its former walled garden, this little-known shrine, pyxlike, provokes passion and religious emotion in the cause of architecture, much as Vistabella was soon to do in a reversal of cause and means. Can Negre reminds me that the pantheon of architecture is without saints; even so, through this structure's martyrdom of abuse, neglect, and, finally, dismal renovation, I think of it as architecturally sainted and remember the story of St. Margaret-Mary. Here, as with the saint's self-incised J-E-S-U-S bleeding from her breast, the incised facade's monogram of the Virgin and its surrounding prayer cries, hails, and sings, curving under the cornice's oscillating line that meets the sky at no consistent point:

scratched in plaster, enclosed in medallions, an invocation surrounded with en-
graved vegetation and birds. The drawn
text wreathed in organic growth leads
one's eyes, left to right, in order to read
the serpentine cornice while its draping
vegetal garlands fall groundward bring-
ing one back face-to-facade with Can
Negre.

Sgraffiti bird

Jujol, Jr., asserts, citing his
father's sgraffiti work in Gallissà's house,
that Jujol never got better at this craft
since his first attempt was a masterwork (see photo, page 5).[1] I
disagree. Jujol's incised plasterwork for Gallissà is studied,
academic, and stiff. At Can Negre we see on a large scale just
how far the architect had evolved his concepts for facade inscriptions using the technique of incising wet, layered plaster
to reveal a design. The figure of Saint Antoni and the surrounding design at Casa Gallissà are deeply (about a quarter inch)
and regularly incised. At Can Negre Jujol brought a lighter,
scraping incision to his designs and a freer conceptual organization, giving them and the facade plane the life of a sketch integrated with his overall vision for the house. While the
sgraffiti in Casa Gallissà looks mechanical, at Can Negre it
flows as if building planes were Jujol's normal sketch pad. It,
and the sgraffiti at Can Bofarull, demonstrate a marked artistic and stylistic development over the work at Casa Gallissà.

Other details at Can Negre further pinpoint Jujol's
mastery of craft: the *trencadís*, the painted decoration and use
of gold leaf in the interior, and, especially, the forged metal-
work of the window grates, the balcony rails (removed), and
the front side gate. This gate, like the ironwork at Torre de la
Creu and Casa Milà, meets its functional requirements with
elaborately forged iron, fracturing and filtering light like natural vegetation. Jujol's designs and attention to craftsmanship
release these ironworks from simple utility and promote them
to sculpture. The metamorphosis evident in this gate is continuous throughout Jujol's work, elevating the common to the
sublime by means of reemploying the most humble, often discarded farm, household, or industrial materials, presenting
Jujol's aesthetic and material control and mastery of detailing

Iron gate, Can Negre

in his buildings, which goes beyond that of any other Catalan architect of this period. His detailing is one important illustration of how the buildings maintain a sense of having been designed by an artist-craftsman, and how a material dialectic is established and used to expand spatial possibilities of low-budget projects.

Can Negre's *tribuna*, perched on wiry, bird-leg stilts over the main door, ceremonializes the main passage into the building. It is Jujol's most perfect integration of *applied* structure, ornament, and graphics into an existing building. It alone elevates Can Negre above the merely interesting projects in Jujol's oeuvre. By opposing the skyward movement of the house's flat facade with a forward counterthrust, it charges the entire house with movement and spatial depth. It is a cycloptic channel both in and out of the structure. To contain the abruptness of its forward movement, Jujol graphically incised around this coachlike structure a swirling *modernisme* sgraffiti design that functions like a whirlwind, blurring the incident of juncture between the two-dimensional facade-plane and the three-dimensional *tribuna*. Below, Jujol further countered the *tribuna*'s thrust by anchoring each of the two stilts with a contoured, triangular, three-seat bench.[2] Each of these seats was perhaps molded to the form of a person sitting in the wet cement and then stylized by Jujol (a technique comparable to Gaudí's for the backrest on the Park Güell bench). The combination of the facade plane, *tribuna*, and benches effects a three-part motion and countermotion: the upward movement of the facade balanced by the outward thrust of the windows and *tribuna* in turn countered by the downward pull of the benches—all contributing to the creation of a vortex above the house's main entrance—an entrance whose doors are ironically nondescript.

The *tribuna* is Jujol's most developed architectural element at Can Negre and, like the rest of the structure, Jujol used it for religious symbolism. It is, in effect, an enormous reliquary; yet, unlike those sometimes crystal containers for the remains of saints, this receptacle contains the living as they view the secular activity below. The central, etched-glass pane depicting the Virgin and child has been long destroyed though

its function remains clear: a translucent symbol through which to view the secular world. Etched upon the gaze of the viewer, this vitreous membrane served as a reminder of the fragile cohabitation of religious and secular worlds. In effect it diffused and overlaid traces of religious symbolism on any view through it—a lucent, subliminal brand.

Directly above, a scalloped and flared cornice fronts a little *trencadís* dome over the *tribuna*, and atop that there once nested a ceramic dove evoking the Holy Spirit.[3] To the *tribuna*'s sides, railed balconies lead from the interior where built-in wooden seats were pyrographically incised with vining ivy.[4] At either side two small bay windows asymmetrically enclose the *tribuna* in single quotes, constituting a tripartite group of forward-thrusting elements that emerge dramatically from the facade.

Can Negre was in critical condition when the city of Sant Joan Despí and the Generalitat (the provincial Catalan government) initiated a partial renovation and stabilization program in 1982 that may have saved the building. This important intervention was undertaken by Xavier Güell, Antoni Navarro, and Gabriel Robert. In 1992 Francesc Xavier Asarter completed a second renovation, which led, happily, to the house being opened as a cultural facility called Center Jujol; however, much original painting and decoration inside and out was needlessly and thoughtlessly erased by painting over Jujol's existing designs. Furthermore, Can Negre is now surrounded by an inappropriate fence hovering too close to the building as it sits in a plaza of cheap and nonrelated materials. Giving no thought to the garden that the house once occupied or the effect of plants and trees on the viewing of this monument, the designers of this plaza created no more than a poor playground masking the fact that it is really a lid for a new underground parking structure. In itself the garage is no flaw, while it is an urban amenity, yet the architect or engineers vented the garage with a huge shaft placed only inches from the rear of Can Negre. Considering the architectural culture that has long flourished in Calalunya, the 1980s' record for fine and innovative design of public spaces, and local care for historic patrimony, the treatment of Can Negre is tantamount to architectural sacrilege. The decision that lets a great building sit in a bleak plaza bespeaks a lavish poverty of imagination.

Walking under the *tribuna* and into the house, one finds the interiors now greatly altered. Still, some important decoration remains. The painting and ornament in the central stairway are extraordinary, both in their humble materials and powerful effect. Jujol's stairs climb in short quarter-turn increments from landing to landing to create a squared-off spiral effect, and he employed decorative painting to subvert the orthographic walls and to enhance the spiraling, much the same way he subverted planer regularity inside Casa Mañach. Over a deep blue ground, fluid and wisping *modernisme* designs in white converge with the simple architectural forms of stacked, truncated squares to envision an ascent and to camouflage flatness

and right angles. These inspired calligraphic swirls animate an extremely simple structure, giving it a visual twirl—advanced by a pinwheel-like ceiling whose radial white beams enforce the spin. It is important to note that the disguise/transformation brings Can Negre's stairways into Jujol's family of circular stairs, an orthographic cousin of the spiral stairways at Torre de la Creu, Vistabella, and Casa Planells. It is an example of the architect's staying within a formal typology while not being bound to specific form.

At the top of the stairway a spacious, front-to-back hall plants a central axis bounded by the *tribuna* at one end and a small family chapel at the side of the other. At the front, on each side of the *tribuna*, chambers exhibit frescolike decoration with uninspired and second-rate calligraphic shields and finials. Yet the doorways to these rooms are beautiful. The vitality of their outlined *modernisme* efflorations, like the stairway decoration, belie the modesty of their materials and again make a direct graphic link to Jujol's calligraphic spatial manipulations at Casa Mañach. This is spatial calligraphy: a flowing and curving valance of irregular swirls caps the doors creating an abstract transition between wall, door, and ceiling. This type of decoration, along with Jujol's already established use of sgraffiti, became basic

elements in Jujol's design vocabulary. Because of their effectiveness
in imposing curves on the rectilin-
ear—a fundamental Jujolian motif
might be termed the circling of the
square—and because of their cheap-
ness, Jujol employed them with only
minor modifications throughout his
life.

The oratory, a retreat from
the rest of the domestic structure, is
a luminous chapel where Jujol
sculpted ceiling corners into
squinches reminiscent of the shells of
Compostella. This symbolic reference to St. James, is, in architectural
form, the support for the polychro-
matic ovoid dome. Below, the

Top: Chapel squinch
Bottom: Chapel altar

chapel's focal point is the gold-leaf altar and its surrounding
wrought-iron lamps, garlands of sculpted fruit, and prayers in
fresco. This intense configuration of decorated fixtures and
surfaces in such confined space yields a slightly garish, somewhat disorienting effect, reducing the accomplishment of individual elements to visual cacophony. Here we have another
glimpse of Jujol's mastery of graphic and calligraphic spatial
manipulations, but here we also can see that mastery in contrast to the incipient romanticism of his figurative painting. If
overwrought, the chapel nevertheless displays the essential
workings of Jujol: fine craftsmanship and multilayering of
techniques coming together to define space.

The literally short distance from Can Negre to Torre
de la Creu and the corresponding great distance between their
designs suggest Jujol's differing approaches in his earliest
works to a new structure and to a renovation. Now, in order to
view the next of Jujol's five major projects and to view them
as a series of related or developing ideas we must move out of
Sant Joan Despí, returning later to elaborate on it as a reposi-
tory of his work.

Notes
[1.] Jujol, Jr., *The Architecture of Josep Maria Jujol.*
[2.] The originals destroyed, the newly re-created forms mimic their mass without the subtlety or softness of the sculpted forms easily visible in old photographs.
[3.] Apparently, no attempt was made to restore this element in the 1992 renovation.
[4.] Destroyed prior to or in the course of the 1992 renovation.

Can Bofarull

In 1914, the year between his designs for Torre de la Creu and Can Negre, Jujol began work on Can Bofarull, another renovation with similarities to Can Negre. Both projects were under construction for the next decade, making it difficult for us to trace where common elements appeared first or to decide whether one project was a testing ground for the other. Each project varies closely related elements: *trencadís*, sgraffiti, and pergolas.

Jujol was called to the site in Els Pallaresos, a small agricultural community near the city of Tarragona, with a modest request to repair a terrace roof. But over the next sixteen years he would supervise a project that he expanded and redefined intermittently until bit by bit he had transformed and built an integrated agricultural complex: renovating and adding new sections to the main house as well as constructing new workshops, dormitories, and garden structures.

At Can Bofarull he merged his architectural vision with another old rural structure, but without totally concealing the original edifice as at Can Negre. From the existing house he preserved the antique facade, minimally detailing windows, building a stone bench into the existing stone wall, and embellishing the archway with a driplintel proclaiming a carved "Ave Maria." The aus-

Can Bofarull, main entrance

terity of the facade transfers attention to the archway and doors, making them this elevation's prime architectural features. This focal point was enhanced when Jujol directed that discarded farm implements be forged and twisted into the door's over-scaled hardware—without masking the fact that the hardware had once done duty on the farm. The main door latch and hinges are crafted from old plowshares—new functions while retaining old forms—giving this portal an antique look of rustic strength imbued with fluid *modernisme* lines.

This doorway leads into the house as well as into a passage to the walled garden. On the garden facade and its attached tower, as well as above it on a new central tower, the architect, free of the facade's historic restrictions, gave vent to his creative powers. Building a low-rise parabolic arch into the garden facade, Jujol supported a second-level, arcaded gallery. On it he constructed an eight-bay colonnade out of rough brick supported by thin concrete columns. This colonnade's silhouette is exotic, giving the farmhouse a nontraditional quality, while not totally removing it from the mudéjar tradition. When completed, this facade transformed the antique building into a two-faced structure: one modified but essentially historic, the other romantic but essentially modern. After respecting the historic nature of the old front, Jujol made no attempt to be guided by it for the rest of the structure.

Jujol plastered the gallery's inner wall and painted it a deep blue, a field against which the orange-red bricks of the arches and the oculi between them contrast. A squat tower at one end of the gallery and a plaster wall designed to mimic this tower's chamfered form at the other achieve balance without symmetry. The juncture of the arcade with both the tower and the mock-tower is materially distinguished in an angled, notchlike transition from brick to plaster that is seen here for the first time in Jujol's work.

The small end tower is one of the most decorated areas of Can Bofarull's exterior. Its windows overlooking the surrounding vineyard provided Jujol with punctuation points for decorative elaboration. A balcony supported by metal brackets protrudes from one side, its wirelike rail mimicking, on each of its sides, the merlons of the tower's skyline, while sgraffiti decoration mimics the shape of the balcony platform on the wall plane below. To each side are chamfered windows

(a characteristic Jujolian device that I will come back to). Windows in the garden and side elevation are surrounded with swirling sgraffiti designs cresting at various and irregular points along their borders in whiplashes, curlicues, and stylized Marian hearts. As at Can Negre we find Jujol using flat planes for his calligraphic-like elaboration. Here overt religious text is replaced with subtle Marian symbols; only the

69

Sgraffiti "B"

Jujol Archive

owner's monogram is privileged with its beautifully articulated sgraffiti "B."

In a sense, the towers at Can Bofarull and the front of Can Negre are Jujol's best planar facades. They provided him with plaster tablets on which he could inscribe his semiotic designs and leave them in the Catalan sun to cure and be illuminated for future generations to read. Today the Bofarull sgraffiti, among Jujol's most delicate and linearly beautiful architectural texts, are slowly disappearing as the Mediterranean wind and sun wear the calligraphic, signing plaster away.

A second, central tower rises out of Can Bofarull's roof, its exterior plaster transformed to exposed brick just below the *mirador*. Under chamfered openings, on each side, are double doors guarded by simple metal railings. Below, Jujol again inscribed the owner's initial "B." Each monogram is Jujolian cursive, and each contains a tau cross in its upper left-hand section. This cross motif and the Marian hearts found below are, by this time in Jujol's career, graphic staples. Jujol, Jr., has stated that his father imbued the letter "T" with a crosslikeness and a private significance: likening it to a geographic reference to Tarragona (cathedral, city, and provence), its patron St. Tecla, and associating it with his wife, Teresa.[1] Here, in the graphic and symbolic merger of the letter "T" and the cross, we are presented with a clear example of the requirement to read Jujol's architecture.

Standing guard above the tower, a sword-wielding angel, with a crownlike appendage rising out of its head ready to receive a flash from the sky and channel it down its camouflaged lightning rod, surveys the surrounding fields. The figure, once a functioning weather vane, is now stationary. Its wings were removed during the Civil War when the owners feared that the house might be identified as a religious institution and be targeted for destruction (as was another nearby project by Jujol, the church at Vistabella).

Below the figure, the roof is surfaced in ceramic *trencadís* with easily detectable plates, bottles, saucers, and a single *porron* (a traditional glass wine decanter). Since the roofs at Torre de la Creu have been renovated, this roof remains the best example of Jujol's post-Park Güell *trencadís* work; it preserves the clearest lineage to the earlier collages that combine broken tile, ceramic, and glass household objects. Except for the Park Güell bench itself, this roof is now his most elaborate and developed use of glass and ceramic collage.

Because Jujol designed, renovated, and built Can Bofarull over a span of years, creating an architectural assemblage in the process, we must view it with its cut-and-paste heritage in mind. Though less flamboyant, architecturally parasitic, and overtly religious, the early segments closely resemble Can Negre, while the later stages seem precursors to Jujol's simpler, more straight-line geometric works of the '30s and '40s, such as the later Sant Joan Despí works.

Somewhere in this development came the small garden structure, said by Jujol, Jr., to be his father's favorite element at Can Bofarull. A series of eight parabolic arches, springing one over the other, criss-crossing, creates an open, outdoor arcade-frame or pergola. Simple Catalan masonry work, interspersed with protruding fieldstones that recall Gothic crockets, gives these arches an incomplete, or ruined, air. Jujol, Jr., states that his father loved the effect of vines growing and crawling up, around, and over this garden work, providing shade while at the same time obscuring and aging the structure.[2] As we have seen at Can Negre, Jujol painted, burned, and scratched decorative vines and garlands in many of his projects, and this may have been

Walled pergola

Dormitory and garage

one of his few chances to design for the real thing. Unfortunately, without the owner's cooperation, this pergola is difficult to see. It is walled in and only its uppermost portions are visible from the street.

Turtlesque iron hook

Like the Casa Mañach chairs, the pergola may be considered an important design link to Jujol's finest work, the church at Vistabella, where the architect more fully and expressively manipulated parabolic shapes and brought the use of crude stone—natural replacements for crockets and acroteria—to full maturity. The pergola may also have sparked its more sculptural and skeletal sibling at Can Negre.

Old pulley as door knocker

Directly facing the pergola is the last section of the house that Jujol worked on, a garage and dormitory for workers. It is less articulated and embellished than the earlier main house, to which it connects at a right angle. Nevertheless, Jujol integrated and maintained a harmonious relationship between his three structural masses: house, dormitory, and pergola. In addition to using a chamfered corner window as a design element and a reference to his angled tower walls and chamfered tower windows, he devised an appropriate rusticness for the newer facades, gracefully providing a utilitarian surface while also making an uncomplicated transition between new and antique facades. By using rough plaster for the walls, by selectively revealing the heavy stone and brick work of the underlying surface, and by exaggerating the windows and doorways with decorative rustic outlining in brick, Jujol created an independent but sympathetic relationship between potentially conflicting structures.

In a similar way, Jujol used hardware throughout the project as a means to compositional harmony. In addition to the farm implements used on the front doors, he created a magnificent triangular screen for the garden's enclosing wall. As elements of overall unity these screens, grilles, hinges, and doorpulls gave Jujol the opportunity to extract the inherent design or whimsical animalesque profiles he fancied in discarded farm and industrial hardware as, for example, when he resurrected an old pulley into a door knocker with a curious animalesque profile or when he turned spikes into serpents. In essence, he developed collage hardware. The result of this design gesture recalls gargoyles and it reinforces a sense that even small aspects of design were craft-worthy to the architect. They imbue Can Bofarull with a charm and a fanciful air that can only be appreciated at close range.

For Can Bofarull Jujol related discordant elements, mass and surface, and built an enclosing complex that looks out to the countryside from which it emerges, more a small community than a simple dwelling. If it is a collage of materials and techniques, ideas and designs, it, like the collages for Park Güell, resolves discordant elements in a considered assemblage that relies on the effect of all pieces working in unison against the disarray of their individual natures or the associations of their humble and often inappropriate architectural nature. As at Can Negre, but different from his work at Park Güell, we can see Jujol at Can Bofarull as a master manipulator of fragments—spatial or material—more aligned with the concerns of contemporary artists than architects.

Can Ximenis

Today we see both Can Negre and Can Bofarull as works of architecture, but most likely the present reality was never a planned reality. Both houses were long-term renovations and Jujol may never have known where or what the next fragment would be. Both should be looked on as composed of architectural fragments that were unified, or later came to be unified, segmentally. The two works are architectural assemblage. At Can Negre and Can Bofarull Jujol is more a large-scale, architectural *bricoleur* than a traditional architect.

The same year in which Jujol began Can Bofarull, 1914, he designed another renovation, Can Ximenis, an apart-

ment building in the City of Tarragona that is situated directly
on the former site of the old Roman wall, which was partially
demolished years prior to Jujol's involvement. This small urban structure, though harmoniously integrated, modestly well
detailed with sgraffiti decoration and handsome woven-metal
balcony rails (similar to those at Can Bofarull and Casa
Planells) may be viewed as an archetype of Jujol's small, urban buildings in Barcelona. So far as extant structures of its
type can, it illustrates the lack of the brilliance and originality
seen in Torre de la Creu, Can Negre, Can Bofarull, Vistabella,
or Casa Planells. It distinguishes itself neither urbanistically
nor as a design vehicle for its architect. Whether limited by the
owner's budget or their design restrictions, structures like Can
Ximenis, Torre Queralt (1917), and Can Brueuers (1918) all
lack the expressive delight, materiality, and creative spatial and
decorative manipulations exhibited in Jujol's best work. These
ho-hum little apartment buildings may be pegged as
noucentisme, though without the spatial spark of works like
Torre Serra-Xaus. For the specialist, these structures and a few
others have elements of interest and relevance in Jujol's ma-
turing career; they suggest that from a very early point Jujol
attempted to be pragmatic in the face of circumscribed possibilities. Never patronized like Gaudí, he saw his few potentially
big commissions fade when clients ran out of money or died; many
of his great works are isolated in tiny villages lost in the Tarragona
landscape, while even his religious patronage came from poor
parochial convents or parishes.

There may be an irony in the isolated sites of Jujol's
best work: owing to their remoteness, the buildings have been
seen by few people, thus partially causing Jujol's obscurity, but
also, partially, leading to their preservation, almost acciden-
tally. Nowhere is this is more true than at his church in the
village of Vistabella.

Notes
[1] Jujol, Jr., *The Architecture of Josep Maria Jujol*.
[2] Ibid.

The Church of Vistabella

From a distance, the parish church of Vistabella dominates the skyline, its pinnacle a silhouette marking the
site of a small agricultural village surrounded by vineyards. Vistabella stands, like churches Richard Sennett
describes "in the center of traditional European villages and towns [making] evident to the eye where
to find God. These centers defined a space of recognition. God is legible: he is within, within the
sanctuary as within the soul."[1] Building with locally made brick and rock gathered from the surrounding countryside, villagers collectively organized, alternating shifts away from their
farms, erecting this signaling structure with
little more than one mastermason, his helper,
popular enthusiasm, hard labor, and, of
course, Jujol's participating, guiding hand.
Graceful parabolic vaults seem to
thrust the four-pronged steeple skyward,
letting its craggy tower emerge from their
intersections at the exterior seams and
ridges of the parabolic vaults
that unite, arching
and ballooning
over this small

Vistabella's fortresslike walls

Ground plan

structure. The steeple is unlike any of the countryside's ecclesiastical Romanesque towers and unlike a Gothic spire, which it more closely resembles. It is a triangulated masonry spike, a geomorphic sign of faith metaphorically lifting the land—the source of its materials—in a tumultuous effort to symbolize the faith of a community as envisioned by the architect asked to express it. Settled now, sitting integrated, structure to landscape, a rural masterwork, Vistabella looks as if it erupted in the neolithic past, its harsh and rough exterior a metaphor for the supplicant's craggy path to spirituality and protection within.

The exterior walls are terminated irregularly, stepping up and falling back, resembling the weathered and often untended terraces of the surrounding orchards and vineyards.

Yet, unlike the terrace walls, Vistabella's are capped with closely spaced, jagged, and protruding fieldstones that serve as a humble version of acroteria. These walls, sheer in face and ragged in termination, gird the interior, much the way the agricultural terraces restrain and define the land. Jujol's walls hold his structure rigid, sheer, and fortresslike at ground level. The thin-shelled parabolic vaults and geomorphic rockery take on a figurative resemblance to the countryside's contours and seem to suggest that Jujol's intention was not to imitate nature but to further and order his architecture

Portico

through natural observation, expressing in design his keenly developed religious faith as geologic testimony and responding through it to the communal requirements and aspirations for a parochial church.

In plan, the structure is diamond-shaped, created by pivoting a square; the entrance, a buttressed portico is located at the plaza-facing corner. The tripartite portals are constructed by cantilevering masonry, inch by inch, up and out, from slightly above the midpoint of the buttresses, forming Moorish-

Main Altar, Vistabella
Insert: Vault crossing bursting into ornamental flames

inspired, pointed archways, thus establishing a zig-zag prece-
dent followed in the portico's frieze and, further up, in the
steeple's cutouts. Jujol joined the zig-zagging portico to the
upper facade with a series of masonry tetrahedrons prismatic-
ally folding back on and out of one another, looking like a
weighty work of origami. At the juncture of the portico and the
exterior walls Jujol began diminishing Vistabella's dominat-
ing and fortresslike stance and started to develop its symbolic
place as a station between life and belief. The transformation
of sheer and hard to undulating, curved, and crystalline effectively making a tripartite evolution: walls to vaults, vaults to
steeple, steeple to sky. A trinity of symbol, function, and material.

Inside, the dominant and overwhelming sensation is
that of a tented cavernous space separated from the sky by a
thin, taut, masonry tile membrane. After moving through the
portal, you stand directly opposite the main altar. Midway between the door behind and the altar in front you find yourself
under (but separated from) the steeple by the highest point of
the parabolic vaulting. From here, to either side of you are
small chapels. Slightly behind you and next to the door is the
baptismal font while, next to it, a narrow circular stairway rises
to choir lofts immediately above the doorway. Follow the stairway spirals, mollusklike, to the roof, and an exterior, narrow
stairway takes you over the elephant-back vaults and up to the
section of the steeple containing the bells.

Facing the main altar you are before a restoration of
Jujol's original, a restoration carried out in good faith after a
Civil War fire destroyed the original. (At Vistabella, in addition to the interior destruction, the steeple's cross was shot
down and the bells removed and melted down for armaments.
Today the cross has been reproduced in concrete and the bells
replaced with a loudspeaker and public address system.) Looking at the paintings while inspecting the war damage, Jujol
said: "The Reds have given them [the paintings] the hue that
only centuries can bestow."[2] Not satisfied with the war's pa-
tina or Jujol's signal of approval, restorers substituted acryl-
ics for the original pigments, giving the renovation a plastic
sheen that too cleanly and vividly contrasts with the remain-
ing original decoration. Whereas Jujol's original works are soft
and painterly, the restoration is flat, harsh, and glaringly rigid.
Even though the restored retable painting was rendered with

great care, following Jujol's sinuous calligraphic lines and *modernisme* borders, its effect is still static and flat, more like a child's carefully filled-in coloring book (photos page 78). Still, the architect's intentions were preserved: the radiant Virgin is surrounded by painted and gold-leaf flames; above her the seams of the vaulting burst into gold-leaf flames, while the interior shell reflects the vault of heaven: deep blue sprinkled with gold stars.

On each side of the Virgin, the wisping blue, gold, and white designs undulate, flowing into spectacular calligraphic inscriptions and prayers. Further to each side, in the auxillary chapels, examples of painting from Jujol's hand remain. On one side, the figure of an angel bearing an inscription floats between stalks of wheat and clusters of grapes, the harvest and bounty of the land. The angelic inscription, though faded, and the figure, though slightly obscured, enhance the stillness of these seemingly oriental-inspired paintings. They look as if Jujol painted them with a dry, calligraphic brush (above and page 79).

The opposite chapel displays a more typical Jujolian graphic device. Paintings here consist of large areas surrounded by irregularly scalloped borders, varying in width and color and serving as decorative shields for inscriptions. These walls present beautiful designs where undulating texts and graphics are freed from linear and alphabetic rigidity, allowing them to hover as though freed of gravity: ethereal, they whisper and recede, providing an appropriate graphic voice for a devotional building.

Looking to the lofts above, it is important to remember that the parish built the church with few resources. These lofts, reminiscent of willow baskets, were fabricated from the recycled elements of the exterior scaffolding, decorated with geometric bands pyrographically inscribed in a technique identical to, though simpler in design than, that used on the inte-

Top: Jujol's original *Alleluya* with grapes
Bottom: Choir loft

81

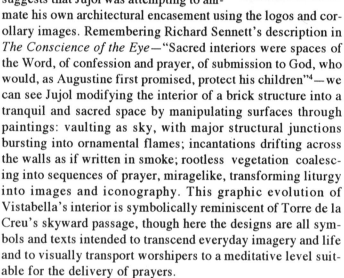

rior mirador seats at Can Negre, and with some chairs and bookcases Jujol built for his own apartment.[3] Today, the larger choir loft is used as a tiny gallery, displaying some of the original lamps and plasterwork that survived the Civil War. And here again, nearly hidden from view, we find Jujol's signature.

Vistabella's interior decoration suggests that Jujol was attempting to animate his own architectural encasement using the logos and corollary images. Remembering Richard Sennett's description in *The Conscience of the Eye*—"Sacred interiors were spaces of the Word, of confession and prayer, of submission to God, who would, as Augustine first promised, protect his children"[4]—we can see Jujol modifying the interior of a brick structure into a tranquil and sacred space by manipulating surfaces through paintings: vaulting as sky, with major structural junctions bursting into ornamental flames; incantations drifting across the walls as if written in smoke; rootless vegetation coalescing into sequences of prayer, miragelike, transforming liturgy into images and iconography. This graphic evolution of Vistabella's interior is symbolically reminiscent of Torre de la Creu's skyward passage, though here the designs are all symbols and texts intended to transcend everyday imagery and life and to visually transport worshipers to a meditative level suitable for the delivery of prayers.

This, too, may have been Jujol's intention for the structure. With few exceptions he typically integrated religious symbolism into his architecture, but none of his other constructions, not even Can Negre's *tribuna*, has such a fluid relationship of structure to environment or decorative iconography to function. And no other of his buildings, except Torre de la Creu, relies on its structural core as the backbone for the integration of form and sign. Here, and only here, did Jujol allow himself a structure nearly as abstract as the ceramic collages he created on the bench at Park Güell; but, unlike the work for Gaudí, Jujol created the structural armature as well. For the architect who continually portrayed writing on his work, architecture would for once transcend writing and hold as both form and message. This was Jujol's pinnacle.

In no subsequent structure, with the exception of

Montferri, the religious sanctuary he never completed, did Jujol attempt to follow Vistabella along stylistic or structural lines. No other of his structures repeats this type of abstract massing, profile, or silhouette. It may be that Vistabella's unique form was an attempt to situate architecture, while satisfying function, in the service of contemplation, or more precisely, meditation and prayer, in the manner of a three-dimensional Christian mandala. If so, perhaps Jujol was developing a hierarchical system where the most structurally expressive and intellectually complex buildings were reserved for religious functions or spiritual contemplation. On the other hand, it may be unique in his oeuvre simply because he never had the opportunity to build anything else like it.

Vistabella is one of the great European works of the twentieth century. It is a masterfully conceived structure where fortress walls encase Catalan vaults with an abstract plasticity seen nowhere else.[5] These vaults, visual precursors to tensile structures, provide a voluminous interior. Jujol's subverting a square into a diamond plan allowed him to place four support pillars so that they would define the intersections of an aisle and transept while leaving triangular niches for side chapels, thus defining a Greek cross within the diamond. He thus manipulated orthodox church iconography in an unorthodox manner, maintaining, all the while, the geometric economy of a square. Jujol broke the tradition dictated by the cruciform plan, violated prevailing architectural norms, worked with the most lowly materials, and created a rough-hewn masterpiece.

Notes

[1] Richard Sennett, *The Conscience of the Eye* (New York. Knopf, 1990), 44.

[2] Josep Maria Jujol, Jr., *The Architecture of Josep Maria Jujol.*

[3] These pyrographic bench seats disappeared from Can Negre sometime between our 1983 visit and the 1992 renovation.

[4] Richard Sennett, *The Conscience of the Eye*, 36.

[5] The technique of building Vistabella's vaults and domes, as well as the domes of Torre de la Creu, the vaults of Montserrat, and the small *tribuna* dome at Can Negre, is of ancient origin, perfected by the Catalans. It is virtually the same method that was employed throughout the United States—before the widespread use of cast concrete—and known as the "Guastavino System," which was brought from Catalunya by Rafael Guastavino and used in such buildings as the Boston Public Library, New York's Cathedral of St. John the Divine, and Grand Central Terminal. Technically, the system differs from traditional voussoir construction in its use of flat, thin tiles in place of stones or bricks. Furthermore, the tiles are cemented end-to-end, often with one or more courses diagonally layered over the first in a herringbone pattern. It is structurally an extremely efficient system—sturdy, comparatively lightweight, and easily manipulated into dramatic plastic forms. See George Collins, "The Transfer of Thin Masonry Vaulting from Spain to America," *Journal of the Society of Architectural Historians*, XXVII (Philadelphia. Oct. 1968).

From left: ground, first, and second floor plans

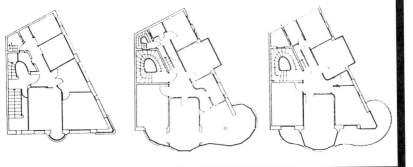

Casa Planells

Scarcely seven months after the dedication of Vistabella on November 12, 1923, Jujol drafted his third and final plan for Casa Planells. His only major residential work in Barcelona, it stands as a landmark in his career, as well as the marker to the end of his most innovative and experimental design period, begun ten years earlier at Torre de la Creu.

Considered in light of Jujol's previous work, his past aesthetic, Casa Planells is an enigma, rendered more mysterious when we know that for two of the earlier proposals Jujol infused the project with motifs closely allied to Can Negre and Can Bofarull. For the second project the structure was to be a monument to the Immaculate Conception complete with a statue of the Virgin. Intentionally or not, this version recalls Gaudí's thwarted plans to place a statue of the Virgin at the top of Casa Milà.

As completed, there is no religious reference or symbolism, and, as related by Jujol, Jr., the architect was not involved with the final addition of the roof terrace and accompanying structure. (This echoes Gaudí's removing himself from the completion of Casa Milà, though it is not verified that at Casa Planells Jujol quit—he may have just been left out.) The roof addition, however, disrupts little of the overall mass of Jujol's structure and does not interfere with the extraordinary vitality of this cross between expressionism and the international style.

When we take into account that the original program for the building changed several times, that the site was reduced, and rental income became a consideration, we find that Jujol masterfully overcame formidable impediments to design his most interesting and plastic urban structure. Had he continued to refine and develop this in mode, he and his career might not have faced the slow decline and descent into obscurity that followed in the next twenty-six years of his life.

Casa Planells is Jujol's only building that acknowledged, in form, Casa Milà, just a few blocks away. By developing a variation on Gaudí's warped surface, Jujol created a structure entirely free of direct quotation, resulting in a stylistically independent work. Remembering that Jujol was a supervisor, and later codesigner, on elements of Gaudí's building, it is easy to believe that he was able to incorporate the master's sense of geomorphic shape, of motion and light into his own work. Unlike Casa Milà, however, Casa Planells is small, less than a fifth the size of Gaudí's structure, as I gauge it; and unlike Casa Milà's undulating facade, which flows up as well as across the structure, Planells's facade is composed of horizontal curves (reminiscent of the Park Güell bench), animated in bands parallel to the ground.

Located on a trapezoidal site, this five-story apartment house appears as a structure continuously varying in depth, a structure modulated by light and hence manipulated by shadow. With its curved and flowing balconies, Casa Planells is poised on its corner site, like the superstructure of a ship, and for this reason its impact is greater than its small size might lead one

Three detail views.
Casa Planells, front elevation

to believe. Like Casa Milà, Casa Planells disturbs the common and traditional urban sheerness of attached neighboring buildings, interrupting and contrasting with the orthographic canyons they create.

The street-level windows and doors make almost grottolike openings; irregular and rounded, they create dark recesses giving the building a feeling more of a cave than a "machine for living." The metal work, too, belies Jujol's subscription to contemporary styles and technologies. Handwrought iron for the gate, grates, and rails is beautifully woven in wide-mesh screens, simple enough to work on either a modern or traditional structure. Interestingly, the balcony rails,

Street level, Casa Planells

in their simplicity, recall boat-deck rails of woven rope, thus enhancing Casa Planells's nautical presence while totally avoiding any similarity to the rails Jujol designed for Casa Milà.

Arched and gated, Casa Planells's principal entry faces the Diagonal, one of Barcelona's largest boulevards. Inside the gate, circulation is guided helicoidally, again recalling the mollusk-inspired stair-ways at Vistabella and Torre de la Creu. Here, more spatially generous, the stairway leads to duplex apartments whose principal rooms merge into one another and into their related balconies or enclosed miradors.

The second floor, glass enclosed and shutter protected, was originally intended as the owner's parlor floor. Its largest salon is supported by a slightly off-center column whose capital swirls into the plaster of the ceiling. The merging effect of column and ceiling is dramatized by the whirlpool of flowing plaster, probably created the way Jujol sculpted the ceilings of Casa Milà: by drawing the swirls onto the ceiling and directing the plasterers to translate his lines into three dimensions. This ceiling also recalls Jujol's undulating plasterwork at Torre de la Creu and the Cine Metropol in Tarragona.

Spiral stairway, Casa Planells

Casa Planells is more machinelike, more akin to the international style than anything else Jujol ever did. Its smooth stucco surface, continuous lines, and lack of ornament are its principal relation to other modern works. It predates Sert's modern Barcelona works and, had Jujol built more along its lines, mentioning both architects in the same breath might not sound heretical. Any further association or alignment of the building with modern styles is tangential, almost meaningless, once one knows that the circumstances of Casa Planells' gestation and construction are vague and that the architect did not complete it.

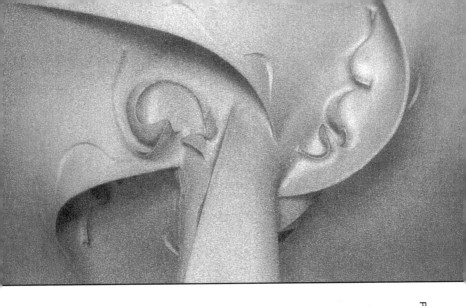

Still, if Casa Planells stands as an exception in Jujol's body of work, it does so as a strong, vital building. Its lineage may be partially traced to Gaudí and his more pliant architecture, and perhaps, partially traced to its client's program changes. If it stands as an enigma among the architect's other works, it may also suggest that, while devoutly religious, Jujol was able to work in a secular, programmatic world. If this supposition has any validity, it raises questions: Why did Jujol fail to produce any future work up to the standard exhibited here? Why were there no further commissions based on this style? No drawings? One simple answer may be that Jujol thought Casa Planells too great a compromise with pragmatic development, possibly a transgression of his self-image as architect. If that is so, it is another indication that politics and fashion by 1923 had altered the design and architectural environment Jujol lived in but not the one he designed in, leaving him stranded between programmed neoclassic buildings, modest renovations, and isolated rural commissions.

Elevation, Santurai de Montserrat, 1928

Casa Planells marked the end of Jujol's most dynamic architectural period. If we consider only the works after 1923, it is difficult to establish a claim for Jujol as more than a good architect. Previous to 1923, however, Jujol had produced five important works; two, Torre de la Creu and Vistabella, are European masterpieces, while the other three, Can Negre, Can Bofarull, and Casa Planells, are regional masterworks.

Because of these five structures, and because Jujol did not abruptly retire, some of his later commissions and projects are important as refinements or tangents of his earlier styles. They further illustrate the architect's commitment to all areas of design and decoration. They are noteworthy for their beauty as well as for their documenting of his later manipulation of space and decoration in even more modest circumstances than seen in the previous ten years. One project, Santuari de Montserrat, begins to illustrate what Jujol would have done with a large structure, while at the same time hinting at the frustration, perhaps heartbreak, he must have suffered when project after project met with abandonment.

Within a few miles of Can Bofarull or Vistabella, and approximately an hour's drive from Barcelona, Jujol began his largest commission, the Santuari de Montserrat. The architect wanted to create a sanctuary whose form recalled the steep, rounded mountains of Catalunya's most holy site, Montserrat, and thereby invoke not only the black Virgin of Montserrat, the region's most venerated icon, but also the topography of Catalunya itself. From Jujol's 1928 drawing several things are immediately apparent: first, the elevation does suggest the

rounded, pinnaclelike rocks of
Montserrat; second, this work is related to the smaller-scale church of
Vistabella, further indicating that
Jujol was developing an architectonic typology for religious structures; and, finally, he was concep-
tualizing and designing projects on
a scale greater than anything he actually built.

As drawn, the sanctuary
and its existing ruins provide evidence that it might have equaled or
even surpassed Vistabella. Forty-
two pillars were to support parabolic arches that in turn were to
support Catalan vaults. Above,
thirty-three small, domed pinnacles
were to rise in imitation of the rocks of Montserrat. The two-
part elevation provided individual yet connected architectural
mass for the two major elements of the sanctuary: one, a small
chapel dedicated to the Virgin, supported on a parabolic-arched
promontory, with a spire reaching sixteen meters high; the
other, the main sanctuary, connected at ground level with the
chapel to the Virgin, was to lift its parabolic domes while supporting a major spire climbing an additional twenty-seven
meters. Had it ever risen above a number of one-story vaults
and several-story arches, the geomorphic mass might have ri-
valed Gaudí's Sagrada Família in structural expression and
presence, something it does in drawing.

Montserrat, stabilized ruins

Jujol began work on this sanctuary using only fram-
ing lumber, Portland cement, and gravel; the bricks were prefabricated on site with neighborhood labor. His structure was
to be completely supported by pillars and arches, leaving non-
load-bearing walls to enclose the church. Windows were created with triangular blocks designed with heart-shaped open
frets. When grouped and cemented in place these modular
blocks made somewhat Gothic-looking frames for stained glass
windows. This application of structural/ornamental prefabrica-
tion at an isolated site is an example of Jujol's concern with
poor, rural construction problems and illustrates his ability to

devise methods that integrated modern, efficient building techniques with appropriate materials for unskilled labor.

Work progressed on Montserrat between 1926 and 1930. After a lack of funds temporarily halted construction, the Spanish Civil War broke out and building was not begun again for over fifty years. Jujol was never to see it resume. Thus the only building large enough to free him from Gaudí's omnipresence never cast a shadow large enough to call adequate attention to itself or its architect. Slowly the unsealed and incomplete vaults deteriorated, bricks were pillaged by villagers, and the project weathered. (In 1987, the architect and historian Joan Bassegoda, the town of Montferri, and the Catalan Generalitat began work to stabilize the ruins.)

During his work on the Santuari de Montserrat, Jujol learned of Gaudí's death, which left Sagrada Família without an architect and his replacement open to speculation. Jujol was widely considered a natural choice. In his 1927 *Gaudí's Artistic and Religious Vision*, Françesc Pujols wrote: "Its [Sagrada Família's] termination should be entrusted to Jujol, who has the ability to take up the work where Gaudí left off."[1] Jujol was not offered the position and no official reason is available for his being passed over. Jujol, Jr., states curiously that his father "had a presentment that once Gaudí had died the workshops at the church would be closed to him," but the son ventures no further explanation or interpretation.[2] From this point Jujol's involvement with Sagrada Família was sealed. And, as if foreshadowing events to come at the Santuari de Montserrat, Jujol's emerging "Gaudíesque" sanctuary would be halted.

• • •

Earlier in 1926, Jujol, Ferran de Castellarnau, and Salvador Martorell exhibited in a group exhibition at the Galeries Dalmau. Jujol presented pastels and watercolors at this gallery, which had been responsible, just the year before, for presenting Dalí's first one-man show, and three years later, an exhibition of rationalist architects lead by Josep Lluis Sert. Even though no evidence has been found that Jujol attended either of these other exhibitions, he easily could have, since by this time he was associated with the gallery and, after 1927, it was located only a few blocks from his Rambla Catalunya apartment and studio. As suggested earlier, he could hardly have ignored such a prominent center of Catalan and international art even if many trends and artists were not to his liking.

Commenting on his exhibition one Tarragona reviewer wrote: "the watercolor *Puesta de Sol* (Sunset), in which our [Tarragona] cathedral's facade, moderately stylized, blazes like a monstrance with its classic modulation of antique gold and flame. This and other watercolors—landscapes, ornamental and decorative motifs—effected with great simplicity and beauty of color—make us wish and hope for a more inclusive exposition by Jujol the painter."[3] This testimony may provide a clue to Jujol's activity and ability to maintain his artistic bearings when, as increasingly happened in the '30s and '40s, architectural commissions became less frequent or more simply decorative in nature. His works on paper, as well as his church decorations, may have provided him, if not with the satisfaction of building, then with enough fulfillment to continue working.

From early school days Jujol had been highly regarded by teachers, colleagues, and architectural employers, not only as a fine colorist but also as an excellent draftsman. Here we can look back to the beautiful sketches of Can Negre's *tribuna* or the elevation of Santuari de Montserrat. These drawings are architectural; the works exhibited at Galeries Dalmau were not. There he showed still lifes, more varied in technique and color than the majority of his architectural work. My experience with Jujol's drawings and works on paper makes me suspicious of the review quoted above. I think that Jujol was a strong and fine draftsman, an extraordinary calligrapher, with a gift for producing textlike architectural sketches and designs. But when it came to subjects that he categorized as art—especially the human figure—his line became sentimental and his composition weak.

By the late 1920s a fall-off of commissions, their rather abrupt qualitative downswing, and the hardship of the 1930s were impossible to predict; surely the lack of important work was not yet a staple of Jujol's life. In fact, one of his largest commissions was awarded on August 17, 1926. Jujol's job was to build a major pavilion for Barcelona's 1929 International Exposition.

In collaboration with Andreu Calzada, Jujol was asked to render a design rigidly confined to the official neoclassic style and greatly restricted by irregularities of the site. The imposed classicism, the fact that many of the attendant metaphori-

cal sculptures were eliminated, that it was badly damaged during the Civil War (restoration has left only the structural mass and curving colonnade) make this project unrewarding to evaluate. Contemporary photographs give no indication of any creativity or brilliance comparable to Jujol's previous works.

By default, Jujol's Commemorative Fountain is currently his best-known work. His other projects are small and isolated. In addition, the earlier works are stylistically diverse and difficult; the fountain, by design requirement, is monumental in a manner familiar and available to a general audience. It is neobaroque and centrally located in one of Barcelona's busiest traffic intersections. In fact, it is less a fountain than a kitschy architectural heap sprouting metaphoric sculpture, lights, flames, and water. Only its architectural mass compels interest. Its tripartite design provides the fountain with three principal public facades where niches suggest triumphal arches. As an urban monument it functionally marks the point where the city of Barcelona transforms itself from working metropolis into parkland, exhibition sites, and Olympic venues.

Like most of Jujol's work the fountain was, and still is, heavily decorated, but unlike its exuberant cousins, it is a sad pile. If Jujol was earlier the collagist architect, the genius of fragment, assemblage, and humble material, he is here the collector, the academic, and the uninspired copyist. The spirit and exuberance of the early works is ceded to cultural romanticism and outright sycophantic nationalism. This is one of his few commissions where secular symbols substitute for most, but not all, religious references. The large pools and sculpture represent the rivers Ebro, Tajo, and Guadalquivir, and Cantabria. The columns are dedicated to the ideals of religion, arts, and heroism. Atop the entire group is a circular cyma supporting a large brazier; burning coals were to signify Spain's constant sacrifice to civilization. Etc., etc.

Today the monument is difficult to appreciate as more than a landmark in the most literal sense, even though it was renovated for Barcelona's 1992 Olympics. Still, we must keep in mind that what we see and experience is in an urban context different from what Jujol planned and constructed for. In his time the fountain was ringed with mosaic pavement and sidewalk, which he designed; benches were provided and pedestrian traffic flowed on and off of circling trams. Plaça Espanya was not the dangerous, speeding traffic circle it is today. Given these considerations, it is still hard to find a spark of genius as seen in his previous works. A heavy-handedness dominates Jujol's use of structure, symbol, and allegory in the fountain, and unlike his use of similar devices in private or religious commissions, their presence in this civic work is pompous and awkward.

Just before designing the fountain Jujol married and returned from a long honeymoon in Italy, his only journey out of Spain. During this trip he took the opportunity to study Roman antiquities, substantially increasing his firsthand exposure to the Roman ruins in and around Tarragona. Before this trip Roman monumentality and baroque detailing had never actually broken into his work, even though it had threatened very early in student projects. If the fountain suggests the architectural direction he would have followed in important civic or even private commissions, then history probably reads better for this project having been his last big work.

Why the Franco government did not find in Jujol, especially with the fountain as a portfolio piece, an architect to express its aspirations in Catalunya is another unanswered question. Perhaps being a strong believer in Catalunya was enough to disqualify him from works controlled from Madrid after the Civil War. Perhaps local condemnations of his position or nonposition during the Second Republic and Civil War were silently but effectively invoked against him. Equally possible, on the other hand, is that patrons may have seen in the fountain and exhibition pavilion a lack of architectural quality, an architect out of step with his time and place, and consequently, in a period of few commissions, they abandoned Jujol to his fate.

Notes

[1] Quoted by R. Descharnes and C. Prevost in *Gaudí the Visionary* (New York: Viking Press, 1982), 222.

[2] Jujol, Jr., *The Architecture of Josep Maria Jujol.*

[3] Ibid.

If time, style, and politics obscured Jujol in Barcelona, if in fact he was passed over by his colleagues and the architectural profession in the Catalan capital, Sant Joan Despí remained open to him. After receiving the commissions for Torre de la Creu and Can Negre, Jujol was almost continually associated with the small city, and throughout his career he undertook commissions and renovations there. A few remain intact; some isolated details survive on others; most have been altered and today are beyond recognition.

Jujol was chosen in a 1926 competition to be the auxiliary municipal architect for Sant Joan Despí, a position he held until his death, though he could hardly have practiced during the Civil War when the town was governed by a revolutionary council. His main project under this title was to develop a section of land adjoining the city. The subdivision was laid out avoiding a standard grid: streets radiated from a circular plaza and were irregularly crossed to form a series of varying-sided blocks. The plan was never implemented, and today a grid scores the site.

In 1984, as a result of Ronald Christ's and my inquiry and with the assistance and permission of the town's city hall, Jujol's Sant Joan Despí drawings were

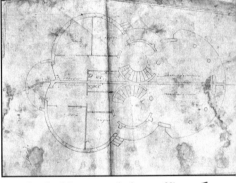

gathered from private citizens, who had become their unofficial custodians after a flood in the municipal archive necessitated their dispersal. We were the first to be allowed to study and photograph them in decades. Because of improper drying and storage, moisture in the folds and creases had caused rotting, bleeding, and stains in many areas of the linen drawings, obscuring or obliterating some areas and details (above and page 44). Nevertheless, what we looked at were the original floor plans of Torre de la Creu as well as a number of drawings for modest commissions, some named with addresses, some untitled.[1]

The simplest of these drawings exhibit Jujol's involvement with every aspect of his architectural productions and illustrate his involvement with even the smallest single-family housing units. In most of the drawings we examined, dating from as early as 1913, some degree of sgraffiti decoration is present; and a number of them display ornate calligraphic designs for their title blocks, further illustrating Jujol's architectural hand as one heavily indebted to calligraphic expression. If stamped, the drawings bear Jujol's Rambla Catalunya apartment/studio address.

Most of Jujol's Sant Joan Despí projects were modest, though among his slightly larger projects are several houses, which provide substance, along with Torre de la Creu and Can Negre, for the claim that the city is a museum of Jujol's work. In the blocks near Can Negre, two important structures show his unique ability to deal with modest domestic structures in terms of planning, building, interior space, and resolution of structure with urban site.

Torre Serra-Xaus is a small, renovated house primarily distinguished by Jujol's pivoting of the second floor dining room, in effect creating a diamond-shaped volume projecting from the main body of the structure with the outermost facet supported by two pylons. This simple geometric maneuver allowed portions of the orthogonal plan to be dramatically modified by the introduction of triangulation, making for angular changes and differing room shapes within a modest residence. The elevated diamond resolves the meeting of structure and street with the creation of a covered entry portico at ground level and a *tribuna* looking out to street activity from above.

Torre Serra-Xaus

This Jujolian device dates back at least to 1918 and the plan for Vistabella and is among his most interesting subversions of simple geometries for the benefit of plan and elevation development. The architect's penchant for triangulated planes, spaces, and shapes is one of his most consistent design devices, even if manifested in so modest a form as a chamfered window or beveled niche. At Serra-Xaus it is complemented by the two small, projecting and pivoted attics, as well as by the exterior, angular stairway.

The Serra-Xaus triangulated *tribuna* may also be related to the curving and hovering balconies at Casa Planells. If so, the relationship may be extended to suggest that from the mild undulations of Casa Batlló through the dramatic rolling of Casa Milà, Jujol was studying and developing an alternate system for achieving undulating affects. Here, perhaps for economic reasons, he replaced the system of curves with a system of triangles, developing facets, instead of undulations, through plane geometry, yet still creating a related system of modulated projecting spaces. This little house, then, seems to place the triangulation at Vistabella in a developmental line with the

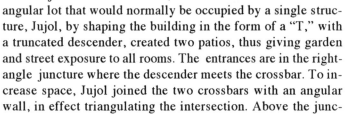

Torre Jujol

planar undulations at Casa Planells and brings two of Jujol's major typologies of form together as a single concept carried out in varied geometries.

Across the street is the small two-family house that the architect designed for himself in 1932, Torre Jujol. Built on a narrow, rect-

angular lot that would normally be occupied by a single structure, Jujol, by shaping the building in the form of a "T," with a truncated descender, created two patios, thus giving garden and street exposure to all rooms. The entrances are in the right-angle juncture where the descender meets the crossbar. To increase space, Jujol joined the two crossbars with an angular wall, in effect triangulating the intersection. Above the junc-

Sant Joan Despí pulpit

ture, small second-story studios rise up to little terraces. Below, compact kitchens were designed for spatial efficiency, providing storage units with direct ventilation through a series of air ducts built into the wall and emerging out of the roof. This modest house, like its neighbor, Serra-Xaus, is decorated with blue sgraffiti designs around the windows. Torre Jujol's inscription again reads *Déu hi sia* (May God Dwell

Here) above the doors. This double house and Serra-Xaus are interesting examples of Jujol's solutions for limited sites, and each typifies Jujol's ability to make the most of the least.

Sagrarium,Sant Joan Despí

Decoration for the Sant Joan Despí parish church was among Jujol's last projects. He created two stone pulpits with flowing inscriptions rounding the top of its tubular form, but died before he could paint it. Here, from the years 1948-49, we see the same sculpted and abstracted handling of text as we see at the 1913 Torre de la Creu, so the church provides one of the most vivid examples of the architect's carrying *modernisme* to mid-century. In front of these pulpits we can still sit in pews he created, whose side elevations recall the helmetlike profiles of the ventilators atop Casa Milà; from here too, we can survey two small chapels: one presents a kind of kitschy folk painting of Montserrat; the other, beautifully completed, consists of a simple, white marble altar, for which Jujol designed a finely crafted sculptural sagrarium and crucifix, elaborately and luminously decorated. Behind the altar, his retable painting is a variant of his calligraphic style, complex, colorful, and beautiful.

Notes

[1.] Subsequent to our original gathering of most of Jujol's Sant Joan Despí documents, Montserrat Duran has catalogued them, and over a period of several years researched and identified others. Her project has culminated in the publication of *Josep Ma. Jujol a Sant Joan Despí* (Barcelona: Corporació Metropolitana de Barcelona Assesssoria de Comunicació i Relacions Servei de Publicacions, n.d.).

Conclusion

The architecture of Josep Maria Jujol is an architecture of collage that includes fragments of vision and faith intertwining the person of the architect with his work. In the best examples, a transcendence of material and sometimes form takes place; in the lesser works, the result is sentimental. His architecture is an art of assembling fragments in, on, and through structural encasements. And these architectural encasements must now be looked at as constructions and placed in a lineage not solely comprised of architecture. Perhaps Jujol is the only architectural collagest of the modern era and should also be thought of along with early practitioners of assemblage. Yet he must still be viewed as an architect, one grafting material, forms, and vision into hybrid buildings.

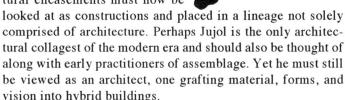

Sgraffiti "S," Torre San Salvador, 1909 (project never completed)

Jujol's art must now be read into and through a more inclusive aesthetic history of early twentieth-century architecture. The five early projects I have discussed staked out new artistic and architectonic territories, even if they never generated a continuation in the form of later, more fully developed work. And let there be no doubt that while there have been and still are admirers, there was no continuum, no disciple, and no consequent Jujolian style.

His architecture was simultaneously his text and palette; more often drawn or assembled than built, it revolved around found and humble materials, calligraphic text, symbols, and connective decoration. Jujol not only practiced architecture, he wrote architecture, and drew architecture onto architecture, and in this sense, his palimpsests must be read the way a sign is read, the way a painting is read when one searches for layers of information. Most of his works are legible to anyone familiar with basic Christian symbols and prayers (which are easily learned by those who are not). In his best works Jujol managed to integrate this architectonic appliqué with experimental structures or experimentally manipulated traditional spaces, creating a mixed-media architecture.

As a graphic architect Jujol was able to obscure or enlighten his surfaces and structures. He was able to mark and encode his works, subverting simple decoration in favor of cryptic devotions, giving to those willing to look and study cryptograms that placed his architectural surfaces not only as screens between rooms and the environment but as permeable membranes between individual users and their spiritual universe.

His facades and wall decorations are reflective tablets, sketches inviting one to join in the architect's faith. Nonproselytizing, they speak to nonbelievers as beautiful modulations and ornamentations of surface. It is remarkable how ephemeral most of his work is—scratched stucco, *trencadís*, and painted plaster—making it even more remarkable that so much of his small body of work exists today. And it is through the bond of materials and techniques that we can appreciate the workings of an artist seemingly limited by the relative poverty of his clients.

If we were to diagram all of Jujol's works, connecting aspects of one project to related aspects of others, the overall diagram would read like a complex network. Further, if one took each intersection and codified it, there would emerge a multilayered chart illustrating a vocabulary of materials, a typology of forms, and a syntax of methods. From this chart it would be easy to see that, with few exceptions, Jujol developed architectural axioms that broke down into units, less sophisticated but nevertheless resembling those in Christopher Alexander's *A Pattern Language*. For Jujol, some of these patterns or typologies would be: undulating or prismatic facades; miradors; triangulated rooms; chamfered windows; spiral stairways; sgraffiti-manipulated facades; abstract ironwork; garden structures; parabolic vaults; *trencadís*; painted decoration and text; and niches for sacred space. This listing shows a personal typology more than Alexander's, but one whose elements repeatedly occur throughout Jujol's career. It illuminates the aspects of building and decoration the architect concentrated on and refined over the course of his life.

From the fractured and broken ceramic and glass Jujol

Jujol's signature tile,
Ermita del Roser, Tarragona

reformed (in both senses of the word) and reconstituted, he interpreted, internalized, and intellectualized the concepts of displacement, disjuncture, fracture, and transformative reassembly into a working nonverbal theory and method for fracturing, deconstructing, and transforming space and materials. Jujol's is an architecture of reassembled fractures sutured (as much as possible) by cylinders, curves, triangles, and tetrahedrons. One look at Torre de la Creu and Vistabella shows this approach and manner as his prime architectural asset.

In a final analysis, the poverty of his materials and clients meant everything. Jujol perhaps required the poor in order to draw the caesura, to reassemble the fracture. From this operative mode, a life and vibrancy was fomented into his great works (even his minor projects often spark with a geometric burst of energy).

It is his fracturing, pivoting, cutting, and layering of simple forms and vernacular materials that sets Jujol apart from his local contemporaries. From the time he orchestrated intersecting circles and cylinders, screwing their vertical space together with helicoidal stairs at Torre de la Creu or spiked triangles, tetrahedrons, and parabolic bellows into a brick tent at Vistabella, he deserved acknowledgment as one of the great Catalan and European pioneers of modernism. An architect searching for a language of form with which he could build his personal vision into techtonic forms of the twentieth century. If he, for a moment, caught the wafting avant-garde winds that also stroked Picasso and later Miró, creating, predating, or keeping apace with their fracturing and simultaneous spatial representations, he did so under a spiritual banner that soon waved in other directions. Jujol's greatness is not on the monumental scale; to find his importance we must look to the greatness in small things, turn to the isolated, the fragment, and the architectural collage. We must now look into the folds of architectural history to provide an intellectual space where Jujol's material brilliance and intricate spatial overlappings are recognized not for scale but for inspiration and beauty, where his building signs, symbols, and texts can be studied as calligraphic architecture, and where the recycled is celebrated not as secondhand but as elemental and primary.

SITES/Lumen Books

Deconstructing the Kimbell:
An Essay on Meaning and Architecture
Michael Benedikt
ISBN: 0-930829-16-6

For an Architecture of Reality
Michael Benedikt
ISBN: 0-930829-05-0

The Architecture of Enric Miralles & Carme Pinos
Peter Buchanan, Dennis Dollens, Josep Maria Montaner, Lauren Kogod
ISBN: 0-930829-14-X

ANGST: Cartography
Moji Baratloo & Clif Balch
ISBN: 0-930829-10-7

Independent Projects:
Experimental Architecture, Design + Research in New York
Anne Van Ingen & Dennis Dollens
ISBN: 0-930829-18-2

SITES Architecture 25
ISBN: 0-930829-33-6

Josep Maria Jujol:
Five Major Buildings 1913-1923
Dennis Dollens
ISBN: 0-930829-35-2

The Narrow Act: Borges' Art of Allusion
Ronald Christ
ISBN: 0-930829-34-4

Written on a Body
Severo Sarduy
Translated by Carol Maier
ISBN: 0-930829-04-2

Borges in/and/on Film
Edgardo Cozarinsky
Translated by Gloria Waldman & Ronald Christ
ISBN: 0-930829-08-5

Space in Motion
Juan Goytisolo
Translated by Helen Lane
ISBN: 0-930829-03-4

Reverse Thunder, A Dramatic Poem
Diane Ackerman
ISBN: 0-930829-09-3

Sor Juana's Dream
Edited & Translated by Luis Harss
ISBN: 0-930829-07-7

Culture & Politics in Nicaragua:
Testimonies of Poets & Writers
Steven White
ISBN: 0-930829-02-6

Dialogue in the Void:
Beckett & Giacometti
Matti Megged
ISBN: 0-930829-01-8

The Animal That Never Was
In Search of the Unicorn
Matti Megged
ISBN: 0-930829-20-4

Byron and the Spoiler's Art
Paul West
ISBN: 0-930829-13-1

Urban Voodoo
Edgardo Cozarinsky
ISBN: 0-930829-15-8

Under a Mantle of Stars
Manuel Puig
Translated by Ronald Christ
ISBN: 0-930829-00-X

Refractions
Octavio Armand
Translated by Carol Maier
ISBN: 0-930829-21-2

SITES/LUMEN BOOKS
446 West 20 Street
New York, NY 10011
(212) 989-7944

DEC 2 9 2023